FUNDRAISING
FOR CATHOLIC SCHOOLS AND PARISHES

TIPS, TRICKS, IDEAS, AND BEST PRACTICES
TO FIRE UP YOUR FUNDRAISING PROGRAMS

⧦

Susan H. Gray

Heinrichs & Gray
Publishing

Order this book online at Amazon.com

© Copyright 2016
Heinrichs & Gray Publishing

ISBN: 978-1944603007

TABLE OF CONTENTS

PREFACE

It was a beautiful spring day and I thought I'd drive over to the local home improvement store and buy some garden plants. When I hit the first stop light, my car was approached by a well-dressed gentleman, holding a coffee can. He said he was collecting money for a local youth project. I gave a couple of dollars, although reluctantly. I didn't know the man and I didn't know whether he was telling me the truth. If, indeed, he was truthful, I didn't know whether I would want to support his project or not. But I was trapped and had to make a quick decision. My decision to donate was based on negative feelings, not positive ones: He might think badly of me if I don't give. I would be rude if I didn't give. I'll give this time, but can avoid him in the future.

About a mile later, I drove past a group of high school girls. They were standing on the shoulder of the road, holding posters and shouting "Car wash!" I drove on. Another two miles later, I pulled into the store lot. At the entryway, there sat a couple of boys at a card table. They were selling candy bars to raise money for a school band trip.

It was as if the nice weather had brought out every fundraising group in town. Of the three fundraisers, only one received a donation from me, and a reluctant one at that. I can't imagine that any of these efforts made much money that day. They were all the standard fundraisers that everyone uses, and often not that productive.

Unfortunately, this is where we are with many school and parish fundraisers. When a parish group decides to raise money for a particular project, the group members typically fall back on the same, tired fundraisers. Someone suggests a bake sale. Someone else suggests a raffle. Few people seem really inclined to come up with a fresh idea or a new approach.

Thus the reason for this book. I have been a professional grant writer for 23 years and have worked in fundraising with parish groups and with an international organization for almost as long. I've seen and studied fundraising projects that were wildly successful and those that were embarrassing failures. I've read many articles by philanthropists and had some very revealing discussions with foundation directors and board members.

Based on what I've learned, I've written this book to help people get off the dreary fundraising treadmill, to stop repeating their fundraising mistakes, and to start building a fresh, broad, long-term fundraising strategy.

By the time you are finished reading, you will know how to evaluate your existing fundraisers so you can either eliminate or improve them. You will see how to assess a school or parish need and how best to present it to potential donors. You will understand the different types of donors and how to cultivate their interest. You will know how to retain volunteers and donors for the long term.

Ultimately, you will begin to develop clever and creative new ways to raise funds for school and parish needs. In the following pages, I provide many fundraising ideas, along with some guidance for those of you who must raise money for particular needs. I want to lead you to a point where your fundraising projects are innovative, fun, successful, and a pleasure to run. I want a parishioner to one day say to you what someone once said to me: *"Your fundraisers are so fun! I actually look forward to seeing what you're doing next!"*

INTRODUCTION

When someone at your church asks for your help with an upcoming fundraiser, there's probably something inside of you that groans. There are many reasons for such a response, but a likely one is that fundraisers sometimes have a poor reputation. Despite many that are advertised as "fun-raisers," quite often, they are not fun at all. They demand too much of their volunteers. They don't make as much money as anticipated. They are not creative or novel. They attract the same, finite set of donors every time. In some parishes and schools, they seem to never end.

These negatives stem from the fact that few people take a long-term, broad view of the need for steady fundraising income. Parishioners, parish and school finance committees, and PTA/PTO groups tend to look at current funding needs or the anticipated needs over the next 12 months. Then they launch a whole series of fundraising events. But this is understandable. They are volunteers with limited free time, and thus must restrict the effort they pour into fundraising.

As a result, many fundraisers wind up being sporadic and need-based. They do not create a steady income stream, and they never build up emergency or back-up funds. They yank the donors from this raffle to that walk-a-thon, and from this spaghetti dinner to that garage sale. If you're reading this and thinking "Yes, that's my parish," then you're ready for a change and this is the book for you.

We start with the basic ground rules in Chapters 1 and 2. These are the fundraising rules that should not be violated no matter what. They will keep your fundraising projects clean and above board. Chapter 2 also zeroes in on the one big factor that's essential to all good and fruitful fundraising efforts.

Chapters 3 and 4 will help you assess your current fundraising efforts. You probably have a few fundraisers that need to be ejected, and you will learn how to decide when they should go. But there are probably some others that could be greatly improved with just a few tweaks. Chapters 4 and 5 will help you examine some of the standard fundraisers and determine whether, or how, to proceed with them in the future.

In Chapter 6, we'll look through some of the untapped assets within your parish or school—assets that could be utilized to draw income. We'll also look at the tremendous pool of talent within your parish. Right now, your parish is filled with people who are artists, craftsmen, hobbyists, and experts in various fields and who are willing to share their talents, knowledge, and expertise with others. Yet no one is asking them to do so. In this chapter, we will look at some parishes that *have* asked and we'll see the rewards that have resulted.

Chapter 7 examines the engine that keeps fundraisers running—the pool of volunteers. This chapter zeroes in on the best ways to attract these remarkable people. It also focuses on ways to keep them on board and happy.

In Chapters 8 and 9, we focus on our donors. We'll examine some of the various donor types and we'll see why some fundraisers attract certain ones. We'll learn why donors abandon certain fundraising efforts and why they are drawn to others. We'll also look at ways to keep donors in the funding loop and provide them with the information they need to remain interested and active.

In Chapters 10 and 11, we look at small, medium, and large fundraisers and how each type calls for a different kind of approach. We'll also look at ways to present the fundraising need to your supporters in order to get the best response.

By the time you finish Chapter 12, you should have an entirely different approach to fundraising than you had before. You should know how to attract supporters from outside your parish. You should no longer see fundraising as sporadic and geared to specific needs. You will have a broad, long-term picture. You might not even use the word "fundraising" any more. Instead, you should see that your parish can become involved in activities that feed relationships within and beyond the parish itself, and that those activities just happen to make money.

So this book is not a listing of quick little fundraising projects. It is not a directory of the thousands of items you can sell to raise money. Instead, it is geared toward helping you develop a broad, mature, long-term approach to fundraising. As you move through these chapters, your thinking should evolve and so should your fundraising plans.

In the following pages, I have included many, many examples of successful fundraising projects. I include these not so you can copy them (although you might wish to do so), but so you can see the thinking behind them. You can identify what makes them unique and successful, and why people support them. Then you may want to adapt these ideas to your own parish or school's abilities and needs.

Now, not every chapter will apply to every parish or school, or to every parish's or school's situation. But ultimately, this book can help you develop a fundraising plan that is diverse and broad in its appeal. It can help you plan for the long haul, rather than doing your fundraising in fits and starts. And it can help you design a fundraising program that draws people in and has them asking for more. Believe me, it can happen.

Susan H. Gray

CHAPTER 1
THE GROUND RULES

"Be truthful and forthright."

Before we get moving, we first need to lay out a few ground rules. Actually, the Catholic bishops of the United States have already determined some of these rules. In 2002, the United States Conference of Catholic Bishops (USCCB) put forth some guidance for major fundraising activities. In that year, the bishops presented the norms that should govern fundraising appeals in all Catholic churches and institutes in the United States. The decree became effective in 2007.

Now, the bishops had major fundraising efforts in mind when they created this document, but some of the norms also apply to small fundraisers such as the weekend bake sales. In general, the same principles for success, honesty, and integrity apply, whether you're working on a major capital campaign or pledge drive or you're fundraising on a much smaller scale.

Here, we'll focus on only those norms that might apply to the smaller fundraisers. Don't worry; these are easy. Just keep them in mind as you plan and carry out your fundraising projects. By the way, to read the full statement, go to the USCCB's web site (usccb.org) and search for Canon 1262. The document is only two pages long.

There are 17 norms outlined in the document, but here we will closely examine only four. The remaining norms have to do with accountability of fundraising groups to their pastor or superior, and accountability the pastor or superior has to the bishop. In later chapters, we address accountability issues as they pertain to the smaller fundraisers you are likely to be involved with.

Fundraising appeals are to be truthful and forthright, theologically sound, and should strive to motivate the faithful to a greater love of God and neighbor.

Never deceive your donors. Never inflate the need for funds and do not exaggerate the urgency of your project. Donors are giving to you in good faith and you should respect them as well as the sentiment behind their generosity. So be honest about the purpose of your fundraising, and once you announce the purpose, stick with it.

Here's a true story of a fundraising group that failed to follow this first rule. They began raising funds that would enable them to produce catechetical materials in Spanish. Once the funds were in hand, they decided they'd create a catechetical web site instead. There are huge differences in cost and accessibility between print and web-based materials. Donors recognized this and some felt angry and betrayed by the change of plans, even though both projects involved catechesis.

Some donors felt betrayed, as if the real motivation all along had been to create a web site, and the fundraising group had been less than honest. At best, it appeared that the fundraising group simply had not adequately planned their project. But then, who wants to donate money to people who are poor planners? The whole episode ruined several relationships and destroyed trust in the fundraising group. Needless to say, it did not "motivate the faithful to a greater love of God and neighbor."

I want to mention one more thing here. Fundraising appeals should not only be truthful and forthright; they should also be above reproach. Some parishes operate Casino Nights and Poker Nights as fundraising events. While these may be fun-filled evenings that make a fair amount of money, you should really think it through before running such an event. They can set the stage for excessive gambling and drinking, and in some cities, they may be pushing their luck regarding their legality.

Fundraising efforts are to be for defined needs.

Not only should they be for defined needs, but everyone on your fundraising team should be able to explain exactly what those needs are. Donors and potential donors deserve to know where their money is going. Is it going to buy a photocopier for the school? Color or black and white? Is it to send the youth group on a mission trip or are they going on a ski trip? When needs are clearly stated, donors can better understand what their money will buy and who it will help. They can see why you care about the need and they can begin to care about it, too.

A couple of years ago, a teenage boy appeared at my front door. He was selling home first-aid kits to raise money for the school gym. I asked him what was wrong with the gym. He didn't know. I asked if the money was for equipment or maybe to refinish the floor. He said he thought it might be for the weight room, but he wasn't sure. I just stood there dumbfounded for a few seconds. How could I possibly care enough to donate to the gym, when *he* didn't even care enough to know what the need was? Clearly, no one had defined the need to this young man, and I doubt he had much success.

The relationship of trust between donor and fund-raiser requires that a) funds collected be used for their intended purposes; and b) funds collected are not absorbed by excessive fund-raising costs.

Notice that this norm addresses the "relationship of trust between donor and fund-raiser." Throughout this book, I'm going to keep coming back to this relationship, as well as to other relationships involved in fundraising. But for now, the bishops are simply addressing the connection between those individuals who are donors and those who are fundraisers.

"That funds collected be used for their intended purposes" has been addressed on the previous page with the example of the catechetical materials. The "excessive fund-raising costs" likely refer to those large capital campaigns and pledge drives that are run by professionals from outside the parish. But the principle still applies to small fundraising projects. You should always take care to keep costs reasonable and under control. Obviously, when costs are contained, your supporters' donations certainly go farther. Also, your volunteers do not feel abused, as their work was not in vain.

Donors are to be informed regarding the use of donated funds and assured that any restrictions on the use of the funds by the donor will be honored.

Some donors may want their gifts to be restricted to certain areas. They might specify that their funds go only to the fourth grade class, or only for altar linens, for example. Donors don't often put restrictions on their gifts, especially in small fundraisers. But when they do and when the restrictions are reasonable, they should be noted immediately and they should be honored. After the funds are spent, the donors should be assured that their gifts were used in accordance with their wishes. In some cases, a donor's restrictions cannot be honored. In those situations, it's best to explain why, and offer the donor several alternative routes for their gift.

Here's an example of that last case. I once was involved in an effort to raise money to buy building materials for a renovation project. One lady came to me in private and said she had really thought about this: she wanted to buy a good, high-quality ladder for the builders to use. She had priced ladders and she was planning to hand me the exact dollar amount needed to buy a good one. This was quite awkward as I knew the builders did not need a ladder. However, her sincerity, concern, and generosity were evident and touching. Furthermore, I saw that she was the type of donor who wanted to cover a specific, tangible *thing*.

I thanked her for being so thoughtful and diligent. I also said that I thought the builders had a couple of decent ladders. Then I mentioned that their wheelbarrow was on its last legs, and that we were really having trouble getting people to cover the cost of landscaping. And the nice thing about landscaping is that you can drive by any time and see what your donation bought. Her eyes lit up and she changed her request immediately. So in this case, the donor shifted her restriction, it was honored, and everyone was happy.

CHAPTER 2
A FEW MORE THINGS

"It's not about the money."

There are just a few more guidelines that you should follow as you fundraise and I elaborate on these in this chapter. I also give you the real secret to successful fundraising.

THREE MORE GUIDELINES

Check to see if your parish or diocese also has fundraising guidance.

Some diocesan web sites have comments regarding the USCCB document, while others include guidelines for fundraisers in general. These will help you keep everything clean, honest, and above board. If your diocese has no such information online, you should still check with your parish or diocese to learn the specific rules about how parish groups are governed and how they handle money. You may find information on such things as what to do with excess funds; how to pay contractors for the work they do on funded projects; and what sorts of things you should be reporting to your pastor.

Don't do anything without your Pastor's knowledge and consent.

Before ramping up any sort of fundraiser, run it by the pastor first. Let him know the what, when, where, how, and why of the fundraiser. Tell him who's in charge of it, and how you're handling the money. This should take all of fifteen minutes, but it's important. He may have a terrific suggestion that would improve things. Also, if a parishioner comes to him later with questions or complaints about the fundraiser, he knows that you are the contact person who can address their issues.

Keep clean and open records.

You must keep all financial affairs open and above board. For every fundraising event, you should have at least two people involved in the handling of funds. There should be no room, chance, or opportunity for money to inexplicably disappear.

If necessary and if approved by the pastor, open a bank account just for your group's fundraising. Always keep bank statements, canceled checks, and deposit slips, and be prepared to provide these to anyone who wants to see them.

What would happen if you were accused of keeping $500 for yourself, or if the group's profits and spending were called into question? Would you have a paper trail with which to prove the integrity of the fundraiser? Could you produce documentation to confirm your innocence? Poor record-keeping will destroy a fundraising effort in no time. Worse yet, it can destroy respect and trust between different individuals and groups. It can undermine relationships and disrupt parishes from within.

THE VERY FOUNDATION OF GOOD FUNDRAISING

The best fundraisers are about relationships, not about money. This is the one thing I am going to pound home repeatedly throughout this book. Fundraising involves many relationships: relationships between the people who fundraise and those who donate; relationships between the fundraisers and other parish groups; relationships between donors and the beneficiaries of their gifts; relationships between the fundraising group leader and the group's volunteers; and relationships between the group's members and the pastor.

Look back at those USCCB guidelines on pages 2-4. Now look at how deeply they involve relationships. The bishops expect you to be truthful. They expect you to motivate people toward a greater love of God and neighbor. They speak of the relationship of trust. They don't want you to blow your fellow parishioners' money on excessive fundraising costs. They want you to stay in touch with your donors and respect their wishes. In short, the bishops expect good relationships to start, grow, and be maintained throughout the fundraising process.

To build and maintain good relationships, you must show respect for everyone involved. You should treat others as you wish to be treated. This all sounds so obvious, but too many fundraising efforts involve abuse of relationships. Groups operate by irritating potential donors, making people feel guilty, or pressuring them until they give. Fundraising leaders sometimes follow no rules of accountability, develop a sense of entitlement to people's donations, and express minimal or no gratitude for the gifts received. They take their volunteers for granted. Beneficiaries forget to thank the donors. Groups fail to keep the pastor apprised of their activities.

All of this leads to volunteer burnout, donor indifference, and friction between parishioners and between parish groups. Ultimately, it results in shrinking income and a general parish malaise when it comes to fundraising.

However, when your fundraising incorporates the building and maintenance of good relationships, you automatically retain long-term volunteers and donors. Other parish groups respect what you do, and the pastor is happy with your work.

Listed below are three "rules" that many successful fundraisers, either knowingly or inadvertently, rely on. And all of them have to do with relationships.

Donors should come to care about the beneficiaries of your fundraising.

The beneficiaries are the children, the needy, the elderly, or whomever you are raising funds for. Donors should have a sense of the need or deprivation the beneficiaries are suffering. They should have hope that the funds raised will improve someone's life. So donors should see your fundraising project as worthwhile. They should be able to take pride in supporting your effort and in knowing that some human being will eventually be better for it.

I'll elaborate on this in later chapters, but let me first tell this true story. A foreign priest came to visit a parish that had been supporting him and his work for about three years. He was speaking to a small crowd after Mass one day, when someone in the crowd asked whether it was better to come and visit his parish or to just give him the amount of money that a visit would cost. The priest quickly said that he really preferred to receive the money.

But then someone else in the crowd spoke up. "No! You should go!" The outburst surprised everyone, not just because it was unexpected, but because of who said it. The man who had cried out stood up. He was known as someone who had often complained about his church's support of the foreign parish. He could never see why his parish was giving money to such a faraway project. Nonetheless, he had recently traveled to the foreign parish just to see things for himself.

No one knew it yet, but he came back a changed man. Now, at the meeting, he stood up. He had seen his own parish's teen volunteers sleeping on floors so the adult volunteers could sleep in beds. He had seen the grinding poverty of the local parishioners. He had seen their faith and their generosity. He had seen how untiringly the priest worked. He actually cried as he told the audience what he saw. Now he had a relationship with the beneficiaries and with the work that was being done. He had come to care about the beneficiaries and he wanted other people to have this relationship, too. Needless to say, he became a diehard donor. It was the relationships that made all the difference.

Now, sometimes donors *are* the beneficiaries of the fundraising. If your parish is raising money to install a new organ, add a wing to the parish offices, or put in non-slip floors in the school, it should be easy to "sell" the project. Just be sure to make it clear why the funds are needed and provide enough information that potential donors have a reasonable understanding of the need.

Parishioners may not be aware that they've had to cover increasingly costly repairs on the existing organ. They may not know that parish office hours can be lengthened if the parish offices are expanded. They might not have heard that four people slipped and fell on the school floors last year. Facts such as these will help your parishioners understand the need for fundraising. As beneficiaries, they should certainly care about themselves and see the need to raise money for these important projects.

Donors should have a positive image of your fundraising group.

They should see you and your group as likeable, reliable, thoughtful, considerate, accountable, respectful, caring, sincere, and trustworthy. Lose your good reputation (and good relationships) with donors and you can kiss your funds goodbye.

Here's a sad story of how a potentially great relationship deteriorated before it even got off the ground. A missionary speaker was visiting a parish for the first time. He spoke of the many needs in the poor area of the world where he served. He talked about needing financial help for his programs for street kids, the elderly, and substance abusers in his town. The missionary speaker certainly seemed likeable, reliable, caring, sincere, and trustworthy.

After his talk, a couple approached him. They were especially moved by the plight of the street children. They wanted to pledge $250 a month for the next year to help them. The man thanked them, then said that it would be more helpful if they gave it all at once. With this insensitive comment, the speaker showed that he had no regard for these donors' wishes or their desire to budget their donations according to their financial ability. He was totally disrespectful and showed that he viewed them, not as caring people, but as bank accounts to fund his projects. All of the positive feelings the couple had for him quickly vanished. His donors, who initially had a pleasing image of him, immediately lost their good impression. The budding relationship soured. In the end, he received only $250 and that was that.

Donors should remember your fundraising events as pleasant and fun.

After fundraising events end, donors should be able to recall how they had a great time, or how they made a new friend, or how they finally met the new seminarian, or how the emcee was really funny. All of these recollections are actually good memories of times they enjoyed with family members and friends. They were times they enjoyed these *relationships*.

Some fundraising experts refer to their job as a contact sport. These people know that the best fundraising strategies involve talking, face to face, with donors. They know that relationships are important.

If you don't believe me, think of all the fundraising letters you receive in the mail. How many of those solicitations actually get a donation from you? Why is the number so small? For me, it's two things. I have no connection with, knowledge of, feeling for, or history with the organization or individuals seeking funds. And if I do donate, I believe they will immediately sell my name to a hundred other organizations. So there's no relationship to begin with, and I expect them to begin abusing our nascent relationship as soon as they receive my check.

I want to insert a true story here to further illustrate the importance of relationships to your fundraising. The director of a statewide nonprofit organization for disabled adults had a good friend who was director of fundraising for a local children's charity. The state nonprofit guy lamented to his friend that revenues were increasing, but it seemed way too slow. The children's charity fellow urged the nonprofit director to try putting on a Valentine's Day ball. His wife had been doing this for almost two decades and it was now making over $70,000 each Valentine's Day.

To the statewide nonprofit guy, it sounded like an answer to his prayers. He called up his friend's wife and they began making plans for a similar event right after Thanksgiving. They would invite all sorts of local dignitaries and socialites, introduce them to the work of the nonprofit, offer a fabulous dinner, and have a live auction. It would be advertised as the "can't miss" event of the season.

The event was meticulously planned, widely advertised, and poorly attended. It lost more than $6,000. Why? Locally, there were few people who had *relationships* with the nonprofit and with its clients. The children's charity, on the other hand, had helped children of numerous local families, including those of the well-known invited people.

The post-Thanksgiving event was not the place to create or build relationships. That groundwork should have been completed long before the event occurred. Furthermore, it took almost 20 years for the Valentine's Day ball to reach the $70,000 mark. That's nearly two decades of relationship-building. It was foolish and naïve for the nonprofit director to imagine he could see such success.

Throughout this book, I offer advice on ways to develop and maintain good relationships. All are very simple and common-sense approaches. By the time you start planning your next fundraiser, you should have them firmly in mind.

Chapter 3
What's Not Working

"They keep selling junk!"

Many parishes and schools already have a set of fundraisers that they run every year. The Women's Bible Study group has a bake sale in the spring. The men's club has a fish fry every Friday during Lent. The school children sell candy bars in September.

Now, if you want to improve your overall fundraising, the individual or group that runs each fundraiser should first examine what's already in place. For each event, they should list and evaluate the positives and negatives. If there are more negatives than positives for some fundraisers, and if those fundraisers appear unsalvageable, then they should be willing to eliminate them.

How to Assess

To do an assessment, you should list the fundraiser's positives and negatives, as seen by your fundraising group. You should also get input from the people who do and who *do not* routinely support the effort.

List only those things that are generally known or understood and that actually have meaning beyond the commenter's personal feelings. So beware of comments such as "That's the way we've always done it," or "Hey, I *love* those candy bars!" or "But Mildred Watson started those bake sales in 1950." These are not positive factors; they are sentiments.

I'm sorry, but none of those sentiments has anything to do with the value of the fundraiser. You cannot let individuals' emotional attachments, personal affections, or devotion to history influence a decision to keep a fundraiser that performs poorly or one that has some kind of negative impact. So don't list such comments, and do not take them into consideration when deciding the fate of the fundraiser.

Now, as an example, let's look at the September candy bar sales. Here's how an assessment might turn out:

Positives:
- The school makes almost $4,500 every year and really needs the money.
- The candy bars taste great.
- The company providing the candy bars is responsive and efficient, and we have a good track record with them.
- School children take an active part in helping the school.
- The selling price is reasonable.
- It's good competition for kids who cannot compete in sports, and the kids who work the hardest can win prizes.
- It teaches kids responsibility.
- It's over in just a couple of weeks.

Negatives:
- Everyone needs to lose weight and wishes the kids would quit coming around selling candy.
- People with diabetes do not buy them.
- Some children live in rough neighborhoods and their parents don't want them selling there.
- Some kids live in wonderful neighborhoods, and their parents don't want them "bothering the neighbors" to buy stuff.

- Some children's parents don't want them selling at all. Meanwhile, children with the more permissive parents are the ones who sell the most and who win prizes. So this puts those other kids at a disadvantage and makes for a lot of bad feelings.
- The prizes they win are junky.

What would you do with the candy bar fundraiser? Keep it? Expand it? Dump it? Improve it? Sell something else instead?

If it were up to me, I'd abandon this fundraiser in a heartbeat. It's true that this makes money, but that should not be the only factor considered. I have three main reasons for choosing to eject this fundraiser. They have to do with relationships, the items sold, and the company involved.

SO WHAT'S WRONG?

It puts stress on relationships.

Remember, the best fundraisers are about relationships, not about money. This candy bar sale is messing with the relationships between children and their parents, the school and families, and big-selling and non-selling children. Although it's making money, it's creating hard feelings at several levels.

First, the parents who don't want their children selling may have extremely good reasons for their stance. Yet they are having to hear from their children all about the parents who *are* allowing it. These parents are also hearing how other kids are going to win prizes, while they'll be left out.

Second, the school may be a bit hypocritical here. These days, most schools monitor the nutritional value of every food item in the cafeteria and vending machines. Many are also having to implement some kind of program to fight childhood obesity. At the same time, they're sending kids home to push calorie-laden chocolate bars. It's a double standard. The school administrators won't let the kids buy chocolate bars from the vending machines, yet pressure them to sell candy bars to their family and neighbors.

Third, it creates tensions between the big-selling kids and the small-selling kids. Often, the big-selling kids actually have parents who are the main buyers or who sell the candy bars at their workplaces. Yet those children win the prizes. In the meantime, children whose parents do not support the candy sale or who do not sell *for* them, feel penalized.

It's selling something that no one needs.

Buyers really don't need the candy bars. Many buyers don't even *want* them. In particular, people with diabetes aren't thrilled when the candy bar kids come to their door. Most people who want candy bars will go buy them; they don't need the candy bars coming to them. Selling stuff that no one wants or needs is about the lowest form of fundraising, just a step above begging. And in a tough economy, it's especially thoughtless and inconsiderate.

Recently, I Googled the phrase "school fundraiser" just to see what would come up. I found many companies willing to partner with schools that will sell their products. One web site advertised more than 3,500 such products—fruit baskets, candy bars, frozen cookie dough, wrapping paper, first-aid kits, potpourri, alkaline batteries, you name it. As I scrolled down, I didn't see a single item I truly wanted or needed.

After that, I Googled the phrase "worst fundraisers." The comments on some blogs and web sites were telling:

> "I'm sick of the candy bars! Can't they think of anything else?"
> "Please! No more frozen foods! I don't have any more space in my freezer!"
> "I'm diabetic. I wish they would leave me alone."
> "I already have a ton of wrapping paper and I never use it."
> "They keep selling junk! Why don't they sell something I can actually use?"
> "Everything is so overpriced."
> "I've bought their gadgets, but they break within a week."
> "For me, it's the magazine subscriptions. Who has time to read magazines?"

So there you have it. The companies are pushing the products. The schools get big percentages. And buyers are tired of the whole deal. Now remember, the best fundraisers are about relationships. When you keep selling products that no one wants or needs, you are putting stress on the relationships between buyers and sellers. Over time, it will become more and more difficult to sell your items.

Little is known about the candy bar company.

The company may be efficient and straightforward in their dealings. It may provide terrific promotional materials, offer great prizes to top sellers, produce outstanding candy bars, and give the school a high percentage of the proceeds. But no one knows anything about the company itself, what it promotes, or how it invests its income.

Why bring this up? Well, consider this. I know a lady who sells scented candles for extra income. She holds parties where she introduces these items to women friends and signs up party-goers to sell them as well. She is a fundamentalist Christian and most of her party attendees are, too. The candles come from a company owned by an entity that most of these women would consider a cult. For every dollar they make for themselves, at least two dollars go to the company. I don't know whether they are aware of this fact, but all of their buying, storing of inventory, tracking of sales, and reporting to their supervisors is helping to fund a group they would find abhorrent.

Although not quite the same thing, you may encounter a parishioner or school parent who is an independent seller of a particular company's products such as cosmetics, tools, or cleaning supplies. That person may be wildly successful and sincerely want to help your fundraising group get started selling.

I suggest turning down such a proposal immediately. You don't know about the company behind the products. Part of the income from your sales is likely to go to that parishioner. And once you agree to sell products with the parishioner who works for Company A, other parishioners will hear about it. You will next be approached by people who urge you to sell the same products that they sell for Company B, Company C, and so on.

Back to the candy sale. Our assessment shows that the candy sale makes money. But it puts stress on relationships, it pushes a product that few people want and that no one needs, and it supports a company you know nothing about. Get rid of it. There are other, better ways to raise money, and we'll learn how to develop them later in this book.

Chapter 4
What's Working Okay and How to Improve It

"Clean your soul!"

In this chapter, we'll look at fundraisers that are working okay and see how we can improve them. Sometimes it just takes a little tweak to move a fundraiser from lukewarm to hot.

The Car Wash

Let's start with the youth group's car wash, for example. Typically, it's held in the church parking lot, it lasts half a day, involves cleaning supplies, lots of willing kids, and a handful of adults. But it competes with automated car washes and other fundraising car washes in town. And for the amount of money it makes, it's rather time- and labor-intensive.

Nonetheless, it has some features in its favor. The youth group *is* selling something that people want or need from time to time. Furthermore, unlike the candy bar sales, patrons know that 100% of their donations are going straight to the youth group. They need not be concerned that their money is going to a company or organization they know nothing about. And, at some level, relationships *are* involved: the kids wash your car while you chat with the adults.

Now, if we assess the car wash—summing up the remaining positives and negatives—it might look something like this:

Positives:
- Makes almost $200.
- Provides a service to supporters.

- Is a fun get-together for the kids, and is good exercise.
- Have learned that asking for donations is more profitable than setting a price.
- Is one of the few fundraisers suitable for kids to do.

Negatives:
- Never makes more than $200.
- Actually takes a whole day, when you consider set-up and clean-up time.
- When the weather's good for a car wash, there are other groups doing them around town.
- Difficult to get adults to oversee it.
- Isn't really patronized very well.

Just to take things a step further, you might ask some of the parishioners why they don't patronize the car wash. Ask them to be totally honest, and you might hear the following:
- I don't want kids I don't know washing my car.
- I don't think they'll do a very good job.
- I really need my carpets vacuumed, but nobody does that.
- I don't want to interrupt my schedule by stopping for an unplanned car wash.
- I don't have the time. I would have to stand around in the parking lot, doing nothing while they washed my car.

Now remember, there *is* hope for the car wash. It fulfills a need and it can build on relationships. So how about vastly improving it?

Have one of the parish men's groups partner with the youth group. Plan the car wash to coincide with weekend Masses. Give it some catchy advertising: "St. Edward's X-Treme Car Wash," "Get Your Flash Drive Here," "We'll Clean Your Car While You Clean Your Soul!" This is making it user-friendly from the start. Instead of thinking of it as a fundraiser, let this event just be something that the two groups are doing together. Then promote the car wash for at least two weeks in advance.

When parishioners arrive for weekend Masses, have a men's club member meet each one and offer to wash their car for a donation. If the parishioner agrees, let him or her list what all they want—wash, clean the wheel rims and whitewalls, vacuum the carpet and floor mats, towel dry, whatever. Have the men's club member move the car to the washing area, while one of the youth group members holds the parking space until the car is done. Assembly-line the washing process, with some volunteers cleaning the carpets before the car moves on to the soap suds. Let parishioners pick up their car keys and leave their donations as they exit the church.

This way, no parishioners have to wait around for their cars to be cleaned. They know that adults are in charge. They can order extra touches like vacuuming and tire cleaning. They find their car right where they left it.

Lastly—and this is big—the youth group and the men's group work together on a project. Many pastors long for activities that get the different parish groups and the different age groups working together. Perhaps this is the beginning of more such collaborations.

Annual Bazaar

Many parishes hold major fundraising projects each year in the form of carnivals, bazaars, or fairs. Typically, these are held on the parish grounds and include such things as game booths, raffles, pony rides, and concession stands. In some parishes, they have been going on for decades. Here, I will describe how one parish—which had been hosting an annual bazaar for over a century—decided it was time for major improvements.

The parish had been created in the late 1800s. Initially, it served a population of mostly German immigrants who lived in the surrounding neighborhoods. The bazaar had begun as an ice cream social and was held every year in August. Over the years, it had grown to include a number of booths where people could buy locally made craft items, some game booths, and hamburger, hot dog, and ice cream stands. But over the last 20 years, attendance had been dropping and revenues had decreased. So the parish council decided to take a good, hard look at things and see how the bazaar could be improved. Here's what they came up with.

Positives:
- Clears more than $20,000 each year.
- Draws people from other parishes and from the community.
- Operates smoothly.
- Has a healthy supply of adult volunteers.
- Draws children, teens, and adults.
- It's easy to obtain donated prize items from local businesses.

Negatives:
- It's sweltering in August.
- The cultural makeup of the parish has changed. It's no longer German immigrants, but is much more diverse now.
- The adult volunteers won't last forever. It needs younger volunteers from the parish.
- The cost of the live band is getting prohibitive.

Right off the bat, the pastor suggested that the whole event be moved to late September or early October. Some parishioners were stunned at this suggestion as the event had always been held in August. But the priest was right; things had changed since the 1800s. We now had air conditioning and didn't need to eat ice cream to stay cool. Any parishioners who objected were reacting emotionally. And remember from Chapter 3, sentiments cannot carry any weight in an assessment.

Next, the committee addressed the cultural issue. Perhaps, they thought, concessions should include booths offering Thai, Mexican, Filipino, and Vietnamese foods. This would be more representative of the parish's cultural makeup. In addition, it would provide terrific opportunities for different groups to interact with their church community and with the public.

The committee then decided that the 7th and 8th grade classes from the parish school, the boy and girl scouts, and the parish youth group could each host a booth of their own. They could keep half their proceeds, but would also have to stay until all the cleanup tasks—including those of the other booths—were done.

As for the live band, each time they took a break, recorded music was played over a sound system. The committee decided to omit the live band the next year and to just use the sound system. They also decided that the physical space set aside for the band could be used instead for some of the new booths operated by the young people.

All of this happened about 10 years ago. Since then, the bazaar has added new attractions and has steadily increased its attendance and profits.

Chapter 5
Beefing Up Some Old Favorites

"Awww."

Now let's look at a few other standard fundraisers. Assuming they have been assessed and will be retained, let's explore some ways that they might be improved.

Six Old Friends

Bake Sales

In general, these involve sales of items that some people may want, but few people need. It's also pretty predictable what you will find there—mainly cakes, cookies, brownies, and pies. And, once purchased, most items will be eaten within the next day or two, so the rewards are short-term.

To improve a bake sale right off the bat, don't call it the Ladies' Club Bake Sale. That's a yawner. Call it the Mother of All Bake Sales, Bake Sale Version 2.0, or Bake Sale IV: The Cookies Strike Back. Include the recipe with each sale item. Also include food items that may be frozen or that can be part of an actual meal later. Offer tamales, burritos, spring rolls, egg rolls, or pierogi, for example.

Run the sale at a time of year when people are too harried to do their own cooking, like around the holidays. Or hold the sale near the end of the semester. Create special "Survival Packages" for parents to send to their college students who are starting their final exams. If it's close to Christmas, offer little gift bags or boxes so people can package up the goodies as gifts. Don't do more than a couple of bake sales a year. If these are really great fundraisers for you, then improve or expand them; don't hold more of them. You will wear out your welcome.

Cook Books

Parish cook books generally include a wide range of recipes provided by parishioners and their family members. Typically, these books are published by companies specializing in cookbook production. Sales usually do pretty well, especially if the books come out a month or so before Mother's Day, Christmas, or a major parish anniversary.

If you decide to sell cookbooks, you can probably increase sales if you include recipes from the current pastor and associate. But also consider including recipes from your pastor's mom, some seminarians, previous pastors, and even the bishop. Perhaps your parish secretary knows the bishop's secretary and can obtain a recipe "through channels." Also include Thanksgiving Turkey recipes from the school's second graders.

These are all ways that you can capitalize on relationships. There are people in your parish who remember the previous pastor as their all-time favorite shepherd. Some will buy a cookbook simply because they know he supported the book by providing a recipe. The Thanksgiving turkey recipes will give it the "Awww" factor, and some people will buy the book because their child's or grandchild's recipe is included.

If your cookbook is in the form of a 3-ring binder, consider following it up with a supplement the next year. Supplements can easily be produced in-house, using a word processing program. My own parish did this a few years ago. We developed our original 3-ring-binder parish cookbook with the help of a company specializing in cookbooks. One year later, we created supplements on our own and they sold like mad. Volunteers gathered, sorted, and proofed the recipes, and entered them into a word processing program. Other volunteers formatted them, being careful not to use the same fonts and design of the original. This eliminated any chance of copyright infringement.

We then photocopied, cut, hole-punched, and collated the recipes. The supplements included about 100 new recipes and sold for $5.00 each. Our cost was around $0.55 for each supplement. Many people bought them as small "stocking-stuffer" Christmas gifts for friends who had been given the cookbook the year before. A big advantage of producing the supplement ourselves was that we could easily produce more if we needed them. We didn't have to project how many copies we would sell, and storing the extra supplements did not take up much space.

A group that is really energetic might consider producing the entire cookbook themselves. Small, 3-ring binders are available at office supply stores. Some have plastic sleeves on the front cover and spine, so you can insert your own cover artwork. Alternatively, you can use spiral or comb binding which is available at many print and copy shops.

For the 3-ring binder, a parishioner who is artistically inclined can design the cover, spine, and section dividers. Copy shops can print these on card stock, while the church or school photocopier can be used to produce the recipe pages. This would certainly be a labor-intensive project, but there *are* advantages. Because you are in complete control of production, you can contain costs. You can print cookbooks as you need them, instead of ordering 100 or 250 at a time and hoping they'll sell. You can continue producing and selling the books well into the future. And you can easily produce updated and expanded versions.

Raffles

Most raffles have some sort of graduated pricing for their tickets. For example, you can buy one ticket for $1, or seven tickets for $5. But imagine expanding on that. How about offering 20 tickets for $10 or 50 tickets for $20? All you're selling is pieces of paper. If you're selling on-site like at the church bazaar, have some of your fundraising group available just to fill out the tickets for the big buyers. Have a laptop and printer available so you can produce and fill in many tickets quickly.

There's one more thing about raffles. You should try to offer a whole array of prizes. Some people will buy chances in the hopes of winning the third or fourth or tenth prize, as they're not interested in the grand prize.

Live Auctions

Live auctions are fun and entertaining ways to raise money and do it quickly. They are perfect for big-ticket items, while silent auctions are ideal for smaller items. Let's look at one live auction trick that that has been used at several parishes.

First, figure out the one item that is likely to draw the highest and most fevered bidding. Let's say you have a parishioner who's a locally famous chef. Famous Chef is willing to come to the highest bidder's house and prepare a five-course meal for up to eight people. With a little arm-twisting, you get Famous Chef to agree to offer a second package for up to six people. You don't advertise the 8-person package, and only you, the auctioneer, and Famous Chef know it exists. So on auction night, the bidding begins on the 6-person package. As the bids rise, bidders drop out until only two are left and it's looking like the lower bidder is about to bail out.

Okay, let's freeze this scene and examine it. Right now, you have two people willing to spend a lot of money. They both want this 6-person package. If the auction continues as usual, you will gain the income from the winning bidder, but you will gain nothing from the loser.

If you had advertised both packages, then offered the 8-person package first, the bidding would probably have stalled out at about the same level where it is now and you'd still have one winner and one loser. Then when you followed up with the 6-person package, the bidding would have stalled out at a far lower amount because your highest bidder was no longer competing and the losing bidder knows his competition is much weaker now.

If you had advertised both packages and offered the 6-person package first, you'd have exactly the situation you have now. But when the 8-person package came around, the glitz of the package itself would have worn off, and the bidding would likely be lower than it currently stands. However, as it is now, folks are feverishly bidding on the 6-person package and no one knows that the 8-person package even exists. So how do you capitalize on the current situation, without losing the dollars that the lower bidder was willing to pay?

When the auctioneer sees that the bidding has gone as high as it's going to go, he stops everything. He calls over Famous Chef who is in the crowd, and privately asks if he's willing to prepare two dinners, and perhaps kick one up a notch. Famous Chef appears to think about it for a few seconds, then agrees. The auctioneer then verifies the amounts of the two highest bids, asks if there are any more bids, and, if not, calls a halt to the bidding. The lower bidder is awarded the dinner for six and the higher bidder is awarded the dinner for eight where Famous Chef will also throw in his signature 7-layer cake. And you have gained the greatest amount of income possible from these two packages.

Sales of Handmade and Specialty Items

As I pointed out in Chapter 3, many people are tired of the sales of wrapping paper, candy bars, gadgets, magazines, scented candles, and the like. But this doesn't mean that sales are out of the picture. If you can think of items that people really want or need, you might have a hit on your hands. Below, I will share with you some of my favorites. These are items that I have seen for sale at different parishes, and that have that extra "something" that attracts buyers. Now, just because they're my faves doesn't mean they have to be yours. These are just examples to help kick-start your own thinking.

- Pillar candles made from melted church candles. These can be made by parishioners in their own kitchens. The costs are extremely low as most materials are donated by the church. (Think of all those leftover Easter Vigil candles!) The candles are not scented and they often have a high beeswax content. There's no overpowering smell and little or no residue from burning.

- Sewn items incorporating old vestments. I have seen rosary cases, Bible covers, bookmarks, and covers for *Magnificat* and *The Word Among Us* that have pieces of old, retired vestments sewn right in. Small pieces of narrow trim make beautiful Bible bookmarks. Wider trim or small pieces of solid fabric make unique rosary cases. Such items make lovely gifts for First Communicants, Confirmandi, girls celebrating their Quinceanearas, and friends who have recently joined the Church. Plus, they give the old vestments a new lease on life.

- Specialty rosaries. Some parishes have groups that get together and make rosaries for servicemen and women who are stationed overseas, or for hospital patients, or for foreign missions. Perhaps they can also make and sell moms' or dads' or sibs' or families' or friends' rosaries. For instance, rosaries with gold links and blue beads (navy colors) would make great gifts for friends and parishioners with navy connections. Rosaries with silver links and maroon beads could be sold to parishioners whose kids attend a school with school colors of maroon and silver. Such rosaries could really hold special meaning for those praying for their loved ones.

- Gift items from Catholic organizations. In November, you might consider selling items that could serve as Christmas gifts. Gourmet coffees, specialty sauces, handmade items, and unique creations from other countries make excellent Christmas and birthday gifts, stocking stuffers, and hostess gifts. They're also great for your own use. Some producers, such as Mystic Monk Coffee (www.mysticmonkcoffee.com) will work with you to sell their coffees as part of your fundraising effort. You might also check out SERRV (www.serrv.org). SERRV works with Catholic Relief Services and sells items that are produced by artisans in developing countries. SERRV will work with your group to sponsor sales where you keep 10% to 25% of the profits.

You might also investigate convents, monasteries, or abbeys that are in your state to find out whether they have sale items and are willing to work with you to sell their products. Many religious communities produce items such as hand lotion, honey, peanut brittle, and hot sauce and are willing to give you a percentage of any items you might sell.

- One-of-a-kind calendars. Around July or August, I start receiving free calendars in the mail for the upcoming year. They're okay and they are things that I actually do need. But they really don't work for me. The paper is too flimsy and the blocks are too small to write in everything I have to remember. Each year, although I have a pile of free calendars, I still buy one that suits my needs. But a large elementary school can produce and successfully sell good, large, sturdy calendars every year. Here's how to do it.

Each August, an adult volunteer uses a word processing program to create pages for a 12-month calendar, not for the next year, but for the year after that. The volunteer then takes her 12 pages to a printer who produces cardstock copies of each page, blown up to 11" x 11". The number of copies for each month should be a little larger than the number of students in the school's art classes. The printer also punches one small hole at the bottom center of each page.

The volunteer then delivers this mountain of pages to the school's art teacher. Throughout the school year, the art students use the backs of the pages to do their artwork. Each student uses the pages during only one or two art classes each month.

In September, students produce September-themed artwork on the blank back of the August page. In October, they produce October- or autumn-themed work on the back of the September page. The teacher reminds them to first position their pages so that the punched hole is at the top. This way, their picture has the correct orientation when it's placed into the calendar. The students are then free to create either from their own imaginations, or according to whatever topic or exercise the teacher is currently presenting. Only a few times during the school year will the students have to produce two pages in a month. This is to make sure that all 12 months are produced during the 9-month school year.

By the end of the school year, there are enough pages to make a pile of remarkable, full color, sturdy, large calendars. Each one is unique and might contain the original artwork of children from Pre-Kindergarten through eighth grade. Volunteers then collate and comb-bind the pages themselves, using school equipment. In October, the calendars can go on sale for $10 or $15 apiece, or more.

- Event calendars. Some parishes produce their own event calendars. These are often simple affairs with standard 8 ½ x 11 pages, comb- or spiral-bound, and hole-punched to hang on the wall. The calendars include reminders of parish group meetings, holy days, school vacation days, and so forth.

But at least one youth group figured out a way to improve on this. They produced a "Dates to Remember" calendar that included those things listed in the events calendar, plus parishioners' birthdays and anniversaries, and parish special events.

First, they gathered the dates. To do this, they made a notebook with 365 pages, and labeled each page with a day's date. Next, they set up a table at the church entrance so they saw every weekend Mass attendee for a month. Parishioners entering or leaving the church could stop by the table to fill in the notebook with their own dates to remember.

For example, for Janie Kirk's May 1 birthday, Janie's dad could write "Janie Kirk – Birthday" on the May 1 page. Mr. Kirk might also fill in his own June anniversary as "Dan and Heather Kirk – Anniversary" on the June 17 page. The leader of the ladies' craft guild could list the monthly meetings on the appropriate pages. And the director of religious education could enter the dates for First Communion and Confirmation for the following year. Each entry, though, would cost a dollar.

Once the dates were compiled, the group created their calendar. Using a word processing program and table formatting, they created the 12 months, then filled in each day's block with the information from the notebook. Proofreading was the next step. Careful checking was absolutely essential here and several very meticulous people were involved. Finally, they printed and bound their calendars, using only the church's office equipment. They sold the calendars all through November and December.

Now, because they charged for each entry, the group was bound to make money—even if they never sold a single calendar. Certainly, no one minded spending the small sum of $1 for each entry. Even if every date had only a single entry, the youth group would earn $365 before the first calendar was even printed.

Like the cookbooks created in-house, the calendars could be produced as needed. Artwork for the back of each calendar page could include black-and-white photos of parish events, clip art, copies of original drawings from school children, a portrait of the pastor by a first-grader, or drawings submitted by parishioners to a calendar art contest.

- Plant sales. Some parish groups hold annual sales of house and garden plants. Perhaps these groups could partner with children in the school's art classes. Students could paint and decorate pots that are either sold separately or with the plants already in them.

Bingo

In many cases, Bingo games provide fun outings for adults and create a steady income stream for the parish. However, it's easy for a parish to become "bingoed-out," where interest has waned and the crowds have shrunk to minimal size. To combat this, some parishes might try alternatives.

- Chance-and-skill bingo. Bingo teams form with up to five players, each purchasing their own cards. The game proceeds like any other game. But when someone shouts "Bingo!" they have to answer a general knowledge question or spell a difficult word or do a math problem within, say, 30 seconds. Their team members can discuss the question and help formulate the answer. If they answer correctly, the team receives the cash winnings for that round. If they do not, the "Bingo" shouter forfeits his winning card, and play continues. If two people shout "Bingo!" simultaneously, both have 30 seconds to write their answer on a card. If both are correct, the teams split the winnings.

- Trivia night. Parishes that run trivia nights report that they are an absolute blast. A small group of organizers creates a set of, say, 60 trivia questions. There are 10 questions on each of six topics. Organizers also set the entry fee—usually $10 to $20 per person. They also decide what to do in the event of a tied score, and they set up tables and concessions for the event.

  Teams of up to 10 people organize, give themselves a team name, and notify organizers that they exist. When people show up for the event, each person pays his or her own entry fee and locates the table with their team name on it and a set of answer sheets.

  The emcee then announces the first topic. He or she reads the first trivia question, and teams are given 60 seconds to huddle and discuss the answer. Once there's a consensus, the team "secretary" writes it on line 1 of the first answer sheet. Play continues until all 10 questions have been asked. At that point, someone from the organizing group collects everyone's answer sheets and gives them to the scorekeepers (usually 2 or 3 other members of the organizing group).

  Scorekeepers quickly grade each sheet and post the scores on a projected spreadsheet so everyone can see where they stand. While the scoring is taking place, the emcee reads through the questions *and* answers for the topic just completed. At this time, there might also be bathroom breaks, drawings for door prizes, and opportunities for people to buy snacks or drinks. Then play resumes with the next topic. After all six topics are covered and all scores are in, the winning team receives a cash prize (like $500 or $1,000).

In some parishes, teams go all out for this event. Team members wear outfits that reflect their team name. People bring their own pizzas and drinks. Players deliberately "slip" and say incorrect answers during discussions, hoping that a team sitting nearby will believe they are correct.

- Spelling bees or geography bees—not for the kids, but for adults. You could charge audience members as well as entrants. You can even have participants on the stage wearing little numbered signs.

- Puzzle night. Rather than playing trivia, you might plan an evening for fans of crossword puzzles or Sudoku. Charge a fee for the evening. Start with easy puzzles and work up to more difficult ones. Decide whether people will work as individuals, couples, or small teams. Distribute puzzles and have everyone start at the same time. When someone shouts "Done!" all work stops. The answers are checked by an emcee and the winner receives a cash prize.

- Exclusive event. Consider holding any of these activities only for people under or over a certain age, or only for women, or only for men, or the high school juniors versus the seniors. Have appropriate decorations, door prizes, and snacks.

Notice how every fundraiser in this chapter either addressed a want or a need, or it built up relationships. Look at the Survival Package for college students, the seminarian's recipe, the *Dates to Remember* calendar, the 2nd grade turkey recipes, the trivia teams, and see how they made the fundraisers a little friendlier. They all brought people a little closer.

Now think about ways you can breathe new life into some of your own parish fundraisers. Ask yourself and your fundraising group what are the things people really want and need. Then examine how your fundraising project can create new relationships or build up existing ones.

CHAPTER 6
RECOGNIZING YOUR ASSETS

"People laughed until they cried!"

Unfortunately, many fundraising groups never move beyond their old standbys. In part, this is because no one has ever seriously examined the whole spectrum of assets within the parish and considered just how valuable they are. In this chapter, we're going to look over some of those assets and consider ways they could be useful in fundraising. We'll walk through your church and school and identify many of the fundraising assets you already have at your fingertips. We'll also begin to look at the tremendous human potential within your parish, but which is often overlooked.

SCHOOL ASSETS

The computer lab

This space is likely to be empty (and thus not generating any income) on weekends, during breaks, and in the summer. Perhaps the computer teacher or a qualified parishioner could utilize the space to teach short adult education courses during these times: Introduction to Microsoft Word, How to Make a Spreadsheet, Build Your Own Web Site, Internet for Seniors, and so forth. Perhaps a couple of teachers could run a summertime computer camp or video production camp for kids.

County Extension Services and small colleges offer such adult education classes all the time, and they often charge fees. The more popular classes often have waiting lists. But there's no reason that Extension or the local college should have a monopoly on these classes. If you decide to run such courses, be sure to offer a reasonable stipend to the teacher(s). Announce each class in the bulletin, in the bulletins of other Catholic churches, and in the local newspaper. (Later in this book, we'll cover press releases.) Set the minimum and maximum numbers of students to ensure that you don't lose money or you don't wind up with an overcrowded classroom.

The art room

Like the computer lab, this could be used during those down times for children's enrichment camps or adult education classes. The art teacher or a qualified parishioner could teach basic drawing. He or she could offer a short class teaching people how do calligraphy for their own greeting cards or wedding invitations. People could bring photos to a class where they learn to mat and frame them. Someone could teach a half-day class on making autumn, Advent, or Christmas wreaths. Again, you should offer a decent stipend to the instructor(s), advertise widely, and set minimum and maximum numbers of students.

Other classrooms

If the school has a room with sewing machines or shop tools or woodworking equipment, you can take advantage of those as well. In tough economic times, Do-It-Yourself classes are especially attractive, where students learn how to sew, do simple upholstery, change your car's oil and filters, or re-finish furniture. If a large church kitchen or a school cafeteria is available, perhaps you can offer classes in Asian cooking or candy making for the holidays. If these classes are advertised well, you will attract people from outside the parish.

The baseball, soccer, or football field

This area likely has fencing around it, and that means advertising space. Contact local businesses and let them know the number of people who attend events in that venue each year. Mention the spots along the fence that have the greatest visibility. Also tell them whether any of the athletic events there get television coverage. Then offer rental space for their metal or vinyl signs at a very reasonable cost.

Space in the cafeteria, gym, or parish hall

The craft group at my own parish has operated a Christmas craft fair for years. A few weeks before Christmas, they would set up tables in the school gym and adjacent cafeteria and sell their items. They had handmade Christmas stockings, tree skirts, candle holders, and a host of other decorations. But a couple of years ago, they hit upon a new variation.

They confined their own offerings to a limited space, and divided the rest of the area into booth spaces. They rented these spaces to local craftspeople and artists to display and sell their wares. This approach had several benefits. Word of the sale increased as the new vendors told their friends. Significant income was generated through rental payments in advance of the sale. Customers were exposed to a much greater variety of items and they met local artists they were previously unfamiliar with.

Think about it. If you have similar space, you might want to run such a Christmas fair—or a craft fair or bridal fair. Or consider a business expo, with parishioners or other local folks renting booth space over a weekend to promote their businesses or practices.

Some church groups run annual garage sales, where parishioners donate their unwanted items. These sales often do quite well, and they're also a service to parishioners who just want to unload some things while benefiting the parish. A variation on this might be the mega-garage sale, where the fundraising group rents booth space to individuals, families, or other groups for a sort of one-day flea market.

The organizers will still have to set up tables, but unlike the annual garage sale, they will be freed from having to collect, sort, and price all the sale items. And they won't have to worry about packing up or disposing of leftover items. Those tasks will be up to the booth renters.

CHURCH ASSETS

Parking spaces

No kidding. Many parishes hold live and silent auctions each year. And some even auction off the best parking spaces in the church lot. The church maintains little signs at the prime parking spaces, saying something like "Reserved for St. Mark's Spring Auction Family." And the winning families are assured of terrific parking spots for an entire year.

Rentable items

Does your parish own a punchbowl and cups, nice dishware and glasses, linen tablecloths, vases, candelabras, archways, or pedestals? If so, perhaps they can be rented to brides who want to use them at receptions that may or may not be held at the church hall. Of course, you'd need a contract that would spell out the rental agreement in detail, and someone to keep track of the items. But otherwise, those assets—some quite expensive—sit there and earn nothing.

The church organ

Does your church have a fantastic organ? Is it new with lots of snazzy electronics? Is it old with beautiful, handmade pipes? Do you have a good organist or know of one? Well, consider this. Various chapters of the American Guild of Organists (AGO) offer a *Pedals, Pipes, and Pizza* partial-day event that introduces children and youth to the organ. Typically, the parish organist leads the program. The kids learn the differences between the piano and organ and they learn how an organ works. The AGO has more information at their website (www.agohq.org).

Your organist could design the same sort of workshop, then offer it for a reasonable fee. Young people could get a chance to play the organ, to try the different stops, and to see what it's like to play the pedals. If there's an organ builder in the area, he or she might loan you some old wooden or metal pipes to examine and experiment with.

Years ago, I attended a local organist guild party. At one point, the host handed each of us a booklet of Christmas music and an old wooden organ pipe. He had borrowed the pipes from a local organ builder. When I blew into the end of my pipe, it produced a shaky E-flat. Then the host told us to open our booklets. He proceeded to conduct and keep time while we all trudged through "The First Noel" with everyone—non-musicians, amateurs and professionals—honking their note when it came time. We were awful. But people laughed until they cried. I'm just relating this to demonstrate that a kids' day with the organ need not be a stodgy event. If it's well designed it will be delightful, word will spread, and parents and kids will be asking for more.

Now, think about the universe of assets within your own parish. List the talented people, the people with special expertise, and those who have fun, unusual, or productive hobbies. Itemize the equipment, useful spaces, and facilities that are sitting idle and that you can capitalize on. Do this slowly, thoughtfully, and deliberately. Share the task with fellow parishioners. Discuss how you could make the most of those assets, how they could be part of short-term fundraisers, or how they could create a steady income stream. Write down every idea, good and not so good. Think about how the good ideas could be implemented. Think about how the not-so-good ones might be improved. Then make your plans and get going.

CHAPTER 7
WORKING WITH VOLUNTEERS

"I'm just glad I caught him in time!"

In the last chapter, we learned how to identify our assets—those facilities, pieces of equipment, and spaces that can be used in our fundraising efforts. We also began recognizing some of the talented people who are sitting in the pews and who might be willing to lend their talent to various fundraisers. In this chapter, we'll focus on your Number One Asset—your volunteers.

FINDING HELP

No fundraiser gets off the ground without volunteers, but sometimes it's difficult to find and recruit them. So here are some tips. If you can use the help of young people, then talk with the school principal, the director of religious education, and the school and parish secretaries. Find out whether the youth in Confirmation class or students in certain grades, clubs or scout troops are required to perform a certain number of volunteer hours each year. Then let their teachers and group leaders know about your fundraising project and your need for volunteer helpers. Learn if there are homeschoolers who want their children to serve as volunteers. Give the parents a call and mention the specific jobs where you need help.

To recruit adults, invite people directly. Some people are shy and unlikely to come forward on their own. Always have a mental list of specific tasks where you need help. One of those tasks might just strike a chord with a potential volunteer. I, for example, do not like to bake cookies, cakes, bread, or pies. However, I'll write bulletin announcements, descriptions of auction items, and little press releases for the diocesan and local newspapers. Everyone has his or her own skills or tasks they're comfortable with. So it's good to approach potential volunteers with an array of options where they might help.

Also, invite the church secretary or office staff to sit in on one of your fundraising group's meetings. Let them know, up front, that you do not intend to rope them in on volunteer activities; instead, you are seeking to tap their vast knowledge of the parishioners. The church's administrative personnel know who the new parishioners are. They know which ones are the doers and which ones are just the talkers. They know who has just retired and might have a bit of available time. They know the people who might be interested in your project. They see dozens of parishioners come through the office each week. They are in a terrific position to invite people to join your fundraising project.

Of course, you can also use the "shotgun method" of finding help, broadcasting your need for volunteers. You can advertise in the bulletin and ask leaders of parish and school groups to spread the word.

LIKE ROYALTY

Once you have a group of volunteers, treat them like royalty. I cannot say this enough. Numerous times, I have seen group leaders and project directors mistreat their helpers. Let me give you just one example.

A lady in a large parish was running a fundraising project that involved a church picnic combined with a crafts fair. One of her helpers had volunteered himself and his pickup truck for a day to haul bags of ice, cases of soft drinks, and charcoal grills to the picnic site. It was early in the summer and the good fellow worked hard. Finally, after he made his last delivery, he grabbed one of the soft drinks, popped it open, and fell into a lawn chair for a well deserved rest. The lady immediately apprehended him, announced that the soft drink did not belong to him, and that he owed the parish 50 cents. When the lady related this story to me, she was proud of having straightened the man out. "I'm just glad I caught him in time," she said.

I guess, technically, she was correct. However, she handled the situation poorly, she ultimately lost a terrific, hardworking, dedicated volunteer, and the episode didn't help her reputation as a fundraising leader.

By definition, volunteers are not looking for payment or temporal rewards. The man with the truck was not working to earn a soft drink. Instead, volunteers come forward for a number of reasons. They love God and their neighbors. They are responding to the Gospel message. They want to alleviate a need. They want to make something better. They feel they have something to contribute. They are generous by nature. They like working with a group of like-minded people.

Unfortunately, such good-hearted sentiments can lead some fundraising leaders to take advantage of their volunteers. They want more donated hours. They expect volunteers to buy this or that item for the project. They ask volunteers to drive around, doing errands, contributing their vehicles and gasoline. They drastically underestimate how long each errand takes. Over time, the relationship between leaders and volunteers can grow sour. Once the word spreads, two things happen. Volunteers begin to drop off, and supporters of the fundraising project begin to disappear.

I've often heard people say they quit volunteering for a certain program or project because "it just got to be too much." My guess is that they quietly bore an increasingly heavy burden until they couldn't take it any longer. Then they gave some gracious excuse and bowed out.

So how do you avoid this? How do you keep your wonderful volunteers?

SOME SPECIFICS

I'll say it again: treat them like royalty. Show that you value *them* and not just their volunteer hours. Whether you're working on short-term fundraising projects or a long-term effort, there are ways to keep your volunteers happy, enthusiastic, and feeling appreciated. A few of these are listed below.

Be organized.

If you are the group leader, show up early for group events. If you are leading a planning meeting, have an agenda with specific topics to discuss. Don't let the meeting drift. Keep people on topic and don't let anyone hijack the meeting with long, personal stories. Have specific start and end dates or times for the fundraiser. Let all of your volunteers know what these dates and times are. No one wants to get involved with a fundraiser that lacks organization or that has no specific goal or ending date.

Allow volunteers some benefits.

If this applies, tell your volunteers up front how they can partake of some of the benefits of the fundraiser. For example, if it's a spaghetti dinner, let them know that they and their families can eat for free. Don't wait until the dinner to decide, as this could be awkward and embarrassing.

Reimburse volunteers for their costs.

Offer to compensate volunteers for their gas and any necessary purchases they make for the fundraiser. Volunteers might feel obligated to cover such costs, but sometimes those expenditures can really add up. Let volunteers know from the get-go that they should keep their receipts and you will reimburse them. Leave it up to them as to whether they follow through with this or not.

Offer stipends when necessary.

Sometimes, you really should offer your helpers a reasonable stipend. For projects such as those listed in Chapter 6 that involve the organist, computer instructor, and art teacher, you should realize that each of those people has a real, actual area of expertise. They have spent thousands of dollars and thousands of hours acquiring and honing it. They are recognized as professionals in their field. You're asking them for help; it's not the other way around.

Give serious thought to the size of the stipend and discuss it with the professional involved. If you're asking someone to run a computer camp that will involve 20 hours of contact time, recognize that the teacher will also need a *minimum* of 20 hours of preparation time. Don't insult this person by simply giving him or her a $50 check at the end of the week.

For these same people, ask how you can accommodate them. Do you need to pick up any supplies for them? Do you need to come early to their classroom and unlock doors or set up equipment? Do you need to be available during class time to run errands for them? If you plan to run their program again at a later date, ask how it can be improved.

Thank everyone for their help.

Always publicly thank your volunteers. Acknowledge them in the church bulletin:

> "A huge THANK YOU to Jack Schmitt for his outstanding Intro to the Web class for senior citizens. Thanks to Jack, 32 new people are now surfing the Internet. Jack's next class will be in August. Stay tuned!"

Also, for long-term or major projects, write thank you notes. Include some of the positive comments you've heard about the fundraiser, or about the calligraphy or computer class. You might also write a note of thanks from the pastor and ask him to sign it. Remember, these helpers don't need you; you need them. Let them know that you appreciate them and value their good work. They are contributing significantly to your fundraising effort and you want them to continue doing so for a long time to come. Always remember that the key to successful fundraising is to build and maintain good relationships. Volunteers want to know that they themselves are valued; it's not just their work that you value.

Keep on the lookout for new helpers.

If your fundraising effort is ongoing, continue to seek new blood. Just the sight of new helpers can give a psychological boost to your long-time volunteers. As I said earlier, your church secretary or other administrative staff can help you identify potential volunteers. They can mention your fundraising project to people who pass through the church office.

Make every new volunteer feel welcome. Spend sufficient time with them, explaining what you hope to accomplish through your fundraising project. Ask if they have any questions and make sure they understand the mission of your fundraising effort. You never know when a potential donor might pepper that new volunteer with questions. Keep all of your volunteers informed of the fundraising results and what the funds have accomplished: "We raised $692.50 at the awards dinner and that enabled the Food Pantry to purchase almost 1 ton of canned foods!"

When a new volunteer asks where you need help, have specific tasks in mind. When someone says they "just need help everywhere," no one knows what that means. Plus, it shows disorganization. Volunteers fear that they might arrive at the fundraising event and have to stand around for an hour while the leader figures out what they should do. Instead, tell new volunteers that you'll need people to cook the noodles, set the tables, serve drinks, keep the salad bar stocked, and wash dishes for the upcoming spaghetti dinner. The cooks need to be there by 3:00 in the afternoon, while other helpers can arrive at 4:30. Everything should be cleaned up and finished by 9:30. There. Now they have specifics. They know what they're getting into and they can begin thinking about where they might wish to help.

Ask for input...and listen to it.

After every fundraising event (or at least quarterly, if fundraising is an ongoing affair), ask your volunteers for input. Find out what they think is working and what is not working. Ask for their suggestions for improvements. Learn what opportunities you've missed. Discuss any barriers to success and how those might be overcome. Don't dismiss your volunteers' ideas if they conflict with your own, but give them serious consideration. This helps volunteers know they are worthwhile and it maintains good relationships between them and the fundraising leaders.

THE PERENNIALLY OVERLOOKED PROJECT BENEFICIARIES

Years ago, I wrote grant proposals for a high school. One day, I met with some moms who were working on a barbecue fundraiser to benefit the senior class. These moms were whirlwinds of activity. One was going to contact the local newspaper about the barbecue. Another was going to get her husband to haul sound equipment to the outdoor site. Another said she would have to come to the barbecue late, but could help with the cleanup.

I asked why students in the school's journalism class couldn't take care of the publicity. And why a couple of the senior boys couldn't haul the equipment. And why the parents were involved in the cleanup at all. It seemed obvious to me that the school's seniors—the actual beneficiaries of the project—should be doing these things. Before our meeting was over, these jobs were all re-assigned and the moms certainly seemed a lot happier.

Whenever possible, you should include the fundraising's beneficiaries as helpers in your fundraising project. Are you raising money for chapel renovations at the local convent? Then have a couple of the Sisters help with your event, or at least make an appearance. You might ask some of the nuns to provide baked goods for the event. Are you fundraising so students can go to the state's math competition? Then have the students set up chairs for your auction or have them write notes of thanks to all of your donors. Make sure they are present during the auction and are available to answer questions from attendees.

Such activities might even stimulate these beneficiaries to come up with some fundraising ideas of their own.

When you involve the beneficiaries, it shows that they are not just waiting for a handout. It demonstrates that this is not simply your fundraising group's project; it is the beneficiaries' project. Their involvement gives your fundraiser more depth. If the beneficiaries are present for a fundraising event, they can talk to donors personally. They can address the whole audience and explain why they need funds. They can probably field questions better than anyone. They can relate personal stories that convey the need for help. Donors can meet the actual persons they are supporting and see what fine people they are. The beneficiaries can thank them individually.

And what does this build? Relationships.

CHAPTER 8
KNOWING YOUR DONORS

"Disposable diapers for a month??!!"

People who raise funds for various projects may not realize that there are different kinds of donors. Sometimes, they also become so fixed on their beneficiaries' needs that they forget that the donors have needs as well. In this chapter, we'll look at some of the different donor types and in Chapter 9, we'll examine ways to build and maintain good relationships with those supporters.

DONOR TYPES

Below, I list seven different types of donors, based on their personalities and interests. Know that most people are combinations of these types. Still, if you're aware of these different types, you might be able to diversify your fundraisers in such a way that you will attract most or all of them.

The one-time check writers

Many people are very businesslike, yet very generous. They want to know the basic facts about the project—the need, the benefits, the state of the beneficiaries, and the likelihood of long-term success. They don't need a lot of details. They can usually assess a cause quickly and know whether they are going to support it or not.

These folks probably want to make a one-time donation and avoid a monthly or quarterly commitment. They like to get in, get the job done, and get out. Sometimes, people interpret their businesslike manner as that of people who are cold, unfeeling, or disinterested. But no, it's just their approach to supporting things.

Givers to specific needs

An example of this type is the lady in Chapter 1 who wanted to cover the cost of a ladder. She was focused on a specific *thing*. These givers are more visual. They like to envision what their donations will buy or how they will specifically improve things. They respond to the solicitations that say things like "$37 buys a winter coat, underwear, and socks for one child" or "$98 covers the cost of a sewing machine."

You've all seen those wish lists. They start with an item that costs only a few dollars, then move up to items that cost hundreds or thousands of dollars. At some time, you may want to include such a wish list as part of your fundraising project. If you do, let me make a few suggestions.

- Avoid using round numbers. Don't write "$700 covers the cost of textbooks for a seminarian for a year." Nothing costs exactly $700. When you say it does, it looks like you have pulled a number out of thin air. It appears that you have not done your homework and just want donors to fork over an even $700.

- Strive to include items that give hope or will result in a positive outcome. "$98 covers the cost of a sewing machine" is better than "$98 buys disposable diapers for a month." The sewing machine tells donors that someone can make clothes for their family or possibly generate some income. The diapers tell donors that their gifts will wind up in a landfill. Now, maybe it's really, really important to get those diapers. If so, let your unrestricted donations cover them. Don't include them in your wish list.

- Show that you are a wise steward of donors' gifts. Don't ask for $1,000 for 40 new library books for the school. Everyone knows you can buy used books online in mint or near-mint condition at greatly reduced prices. Requests like this just make you look greedy and indicate that you have little respect for donors' gifts.

Givers of specific items

These are the visual people who are more hands-on. They like to be a little more actively involved in the project, and have a bit more sense of a relationship with the beneficiaries. They want to do something other than writing a check. Many of them like to shop for specific items while they imagine how their gifts might be used.

These donors respond well to specific, itemized wish lists. You might want to post such lists monthly in your parish bulletin. An example would be:

> **School is starting soon and we need:** 50 reams of white, 20-pound letter-size paper; 12 toner cartridges for HP 1006 laser printers (recycled cartridges are fine); 150 plain Manila folders, letter-size; 20 cans Ajax cleanser; 16 pairs, medium-size heavy-duty dishwashing gloves. For more information, call Cassie at the school office: 555-2468.

Now, you might wind up with 60 cans of cleanser and only 11 reams of paper, but so what? It's cleanser and paper you didn't have before.

Givers to specific individuals

These donors value the relationships they might have with their beneficiaries. They are the people who sponsor a certain child's tuition or "adopt" a seminarian. They often pray for and correspond with the beneficiary and may send additional gifts or checks throughout the course of their sponsorship.

Givers of talent

We Catholics often run fundraising projects or capital campaigns urging people to give of their "time, talent, and treasure." The trouble is that we seldom offer opportunities for people to give of their talents. We overlook the enormous wealth of skills, expertise, talent, and willing souls sitting out in the pews.

Some folks may really want to contribute to your fundraiser, but they just don't have the cash, or they feel that their time will not be well spent. Never overlook these good people. Perhaps they can serve as volunteer contributors of their expertise and talent, like the organist in Chapter 6. Let me tell you about a couple of great fundraisers that got a lot of people together who were willing to give of their time and talent. Parish names have been changed, but these events really happened.

- Several people at St. Mary's parish had volunteered from time to time with Habitat for Humanity. They saw how the organization operated and they noted the things that made work weekends run smoothly. Then they came to the parish council and suggested that the parish build a house and sell it. The house should be in a nice neighborhood where homes sold quickly. The group mentioned that they had already spoken to many of the talented and experienced parishioners who might be involved, and that they thought it was a great idea. The pastor, parish council, and diocesan building committee agreed to the idea and the church bought the land.

St. Mary's was a large parish with carpenters, plumbers, building contractors, realtors, an interior designer, and many other gifted individuals in the congregation. Several people were great organizers and they worked together to run the project and keep things on schedule. It took several months to build the house, but almost all of the labor and materials were donated. College students painted the rooms. Confirmation kids did cleanup. The ladies' group provided lunch and drinks every work day. Some people just spent their time running errands and picking up supplies for the workers. When the project was finished, there was a huge party at the house for all involved. One real estate agent offered to sell the house without commission, and in the end, the parish profited almost $140,000.

Now, there's no doubt this was a ton of work and it had to be extremely well organized. But people fell into the routine of working on Saturdays. They saw major progress every weekend. Someone fed them lunch and someone else ran their errands. They sensed that they were appreciated. Everyone knew this project had an end point. Parish groups worked together. And many new relationships were formed.

- Immaculate Conception parish was much smaller than St. Mary's and one of its groups was devoted to raising money for the local pro-life center. They decided to run a project that capitalized on the talent and skills of the parishioners. The group put a flyer in the bulletin, asking for teachers for Immaculate Conception University, or ICU. They asked for submissions from volunteers who wanted to teach any sort of class. The volunteers should describe their class, the day(s) and time(s) for class meetings, and the cost. The church hall and its adjacent meeting rooms were available to the volunteers from 9:00 to 5:00, Monday through Saturday, so all classes could meet there.

Within a couple of weeks, the fundraising group had received offers to teach American Sign Language, basic self-defense, how to make egg rolls, auto maintenance, public speaking, basic sewing techniques, and more. The group then organized and printed a "class schedule" and included it with the bulletin.

The local newspaper and diocesan papers ran articles about the ICU and its upcoming classes. The teachers also told their friends about it and many of the "students" were people from outside the parish. The fundraising group served as organizers, but the teachers did the work. Participants reported later that they really enjoyed the classes and they were glad to meet parishioners they never knew before. So—you know—relationships.

The detail people

Back to the different donor types. The detail people want to know everything before they donate. They want to know how you decided that $700 buys a seminarian's books, whether the seminarian is buying any books on his own, when the seminarian will be ordained, where he is studying, how much of their money actually reaches him, and how much is going into fundraising administrative costs. The detail people are not trying to aggravate anyone, but they do want assurance that someone asking for their money is honest and knows what he or she is talking about.

The grouches

I like to think of the grouches as the people who aren't on board *yet*. These folks may want nothing to do with your fundraising effort, may think it's totally foolish, and may even ridicule it when talking to other parishioners. They might just remain in grouch mode forever. But, I assure you, at least a few of them are staunch supporters waiting to blossom.

A true story. Sean was the leader of a parish men's group that was often raising money for needy children in the local area. I was in a fundraising group in the same parish that raised money for an overseas mission. Sean saw us as competitors for a limited pot of money. He'd see me after Mass and start asking why I wanted money for people far away when there were people right under our noses who needed help.

I could deal with Sean okay. But the trouble was, for some of our fundraising activities, we needed to borrow equipment and a facility owned by the men's group, which Sean led. So how did we handle this? Well, for each event, we specifically invited the men's club members to attend. We cleaned their facility from top to bottom at the end of these events. We left the place with more sodas, coffee, paper towels, and dish soap than the men had to begin with. We left a note for Sean, thanking him and the club for the use of their space. We told him that the money we raised enabled us to provide milk and formula for orphaned infants who were previously drinking sugared water from their bottles. One would say that we poured it on thick.

But slowly, Sean's heart began to turn. He saw that we didn't wreck the facility. He couldn't ignore that some members of the men's club were married to members of our group. He realized that children are children, whether they're local or not. And in time, Sean began to offer the facility and even ask how he could accommodate us. In turn, we found some ways to help *his* fundraising efforts. This all took patience, kindness, and prayer, but Sean the grouch eventually became Sean the ardent supporter.

The never donors

Okay, here's the group you will never reach. While it may be tempting to be aggravated with them, please don't be. Actually, they may have good reasons for not supporting your effort. You should keep in mind that some people are simply unable to contribute. They may be going through hard times or they may already be over-extended from tough times in the past. They might be dealing with family or medical problems you are not aware of and their minds just aren't on fundraising projects.

Also, remember that your crusade cannot be everyone's crusade. Sure, fundraising for your project is important. But some non-donors might be totally wrapped up in different, equally or more important efforts.

WHY DO WE CARE?

Now, why do we care that there are all these different types of donors? We care for two reasons. First, if we know we'll likely encounter these different types, we will know how to address their issues, answer their questions, and respond to their needs. We will realize that not everyone wants to just write us a check. We can anticipate that someone will want to buy specific items to help us. And we can know to expect some grouches and that we must have charitable hearts to receive them.

Second, we don't want to overlook any potential donors. If all of our fundraising seeks to attract only the check-writers, we will miss out on those who would rather "adopt" beneficiaries. We will lose those who have plenty of time and talent to share. We will alienate the grouches for good.

Of course, it's impossible to run one single fundraising event that will attract all donor types. But if your fundraising activities are ongoing, you should vary them enough to include the whole spectrum of potential donors.

A REAL-LIFE SITUATION

Now let's look at one situation and see how to attract as many different donor types as possible.

The budget for the upcoming school year has been drawn up and school officials expect a shortfall of $48,462. Unless you're in a large parish, it's unlikely that this amount will be raised through just one fundraising event. So you need to plan several. You might plan a mix of one-shot affairs with ongoing activities. Also, the fundraisers should differ enough that they would attract most or all of the different types of donors.

Avoid the small fundraisers that will garner only a few hundred dollars. When you host too many small events, people quit paying attention. Later on, they can rightly ask, "Are you *still* raising money for *that*?" Your cause just becomes part of the background noise in everyone's life. Instead, you should run a minimum number of events, such as those listed below.

Sponsorship opportunities

Present an array of sponsorship opportunities for donors. Let them choose to sponsor a scholarship or partial scholarship for one child for a year. Also make classroom sponsorships available, where people can contribute $250 or $500 to the art classroom or the science lab or the library. Have school children write notes of appreciation to the sponsors. Kids in art classes could design their own thank you cards. Other children could write notes that thank the library sponsors and perhaps tell them which books they just finished reading.

Maybe a donor would prefer to sponsor a school week for $5,000. If the donor allows it, call that week by his or her name—Bob Smith Week—and invite Bob and his family to visit the school one day, tour it, and eat in the cafeteria. Put up a kid-made poster at the school's entrance announcing Bob Smith Week, and welcome him on the school's outdoor marquee. At the end of the visit, give Bob a big oversized, thank you card that has been signed by the school kids.

Even if Bob doesn't want to visit, giving him a photo of the marquee plus the oversize card would be a nice gesture. It would be personal and something of a relationship-builder.

Wish lists

Post wish lists in the church vestibule and in the school office and let people sign up to buy different items. Clearly label each list in big print so people can find their preferred list easily: Office Supplies, Kitchen Supplies, Library Books, Computer Equipment. No item is too small or too large for these lists. I know of a high school that received an entire art studio, including a kiln, from a deceased woman's estate, simply because they posted a wish list asking for art supplies. No one would have donated that whole studio unless they knew the school was looking for such materials.

Auctions

Run a silent auction and a live auction simultaneously in one night. Offer all sorts of free food and drinks. Make sure your pastor announces this and also appears at the auction. Advertise it as the "Over the Top" event, which will push the fundraising effort well past the goal of $48,462. Let the auctions include services as well as specific items. Print up and distribute in advance a list of those things which will appear in the live auction. Write clever, brief descriptions of each one, making sure you convey the idea that this will be a fun event:

> **Mahogany Desk Set.** Still using an old cafeteria table for your office desk? Want a new desk that shows how successful you are? Or maybe one that lets you *pretend* you're successful? Then check out this fabulous 60" x 32" solid wood 6-drawer desk with matching chair from King Furniture. Bidding starts at $200.

> **Turkey Dinner for 12.** If you can't take another holiday of Aunt Millie's cooking, invite her to your place for a deep-fried 15-pound Thanksgiving turkey. Four big, mouth-watering side dishes are included with this dinner prepared by Lily's Restaurant in the Heights. Bidding starts at $50.

In these 3 approaches—sponsorships, wish lists, and auctions—you will attract every type of active donor I've listed. Not only that, but at some level you will have laid the foundation for some long-term relationships. And you will have kept your fundraising activities to a minimum.

Chapter 9
Cultivating Donor Relationships

"I wish you could hear what I'm hearing!"

In previous chapters, we learned how to treat volunteers to keep them happy. We've also learned about the different types of donors. Now, let's focus on how to treat donors fairly and keep them happy as well.

What We Do Wrong

Over the years, I have read a number of articles that were written by philanthropists. These articles have presented the thinking, the goals, the concerns, the fears, and the complaints from individuals who are major donors to various programs. Among the many things I've learned from these people, is that they are often poorly treated by the recipients and beneficiaries of their generosity.

This would be shocking to me, but I have seen it myself in the grant world. Organizations receive grants and never write a single note of thanks. They don't even let the donor know that his $30,000 check arrived safely at the organization's office. They fail to provide follow-up or final reports to tell a donor how her money was used, or how anyone benefitted from her gift. They receive a grant earmarked for one project, then apply it to a completely different project. Oftentimes, it seems, recipients have a take-their-money-and-run attitude toward donors.

The problem at the base of all of this bad behavior is that recipients do not realize that donors are people, too. Someone who gives your organization $10,000 may have decided not to leave that amount to their kids, not to spend it on a new swimming pool this year, or not to go on that Hawaiian vacation next winter.

Instead, they have searched their hearts and have chosen to give their money to your fundraising effort. They want to help needy families or disabled adults just like you do. Perhaps they've seen the leaky roof at the church or the poor insulation at the school and want to fix things just like your fundraising group is striving to do. They truly share your vision, and the best way they can help is by writing a check. They're counting on you to use their funds wisely to improve some situation. They deserve not only your genuine thanks, but also your respect.

It's been said that donors want to plant a seed and come back later and see the tree. Too often, though, recipients take these good donors for granted. They don't bother telling them what became of their seed money or that the tree is even growing. They completely abuse their donor relationships.

THANKS AND NO THANKS

Sending a letter of thanks is the very least you can do for your donors. But incredibly, one of the leading complaints of large donors is that they never receive any thanks letter at all.

A thank you note accomplishes three things. It lets a donor know that you are grateful. It informs them that their check safely reached your fundraising office. And it shows the donor that you are a responsible person who believes in accountability.

Very small donations do not call for letters of thanks. But larger ones, as well as major donations of time and talent, certainly do.

Also, it doesn't hurt to add a personalized hand-written note at the bottom of a thanks letter:

> "Thanks again, Mrs. Li. Your $2,000 donation enabled us to start the project a week earlier than planned!"

> "Wow, Jim, I wish you could hear what I'm hearing. Just today, someone told me he saved over $350 by using what he learned in your floor tiling class."

Such notes aren't just appreciative. They help sustain the donor's connection with the fundraising's beneficiaries, with the fundraising group, or with others the donors met through a fundraising project. In other words, they help to strengthen relationships.

Now, some donors specifically ask not to be recognized in any way. They have reasons for making this request, *so honor it*. These donors may have spouses or children who disagree with their giving practices, or who do not care for the recipient organizations, so they prefer their giving to be private. The donors may not want their name out in public as this may attract unscrupulous individuals seeking money.

So do not send the thanks letter. Do not add them to a mailing list. Do not send them updates on the project they helped fund. Do not mention them in press releases. Do not damage the trusting relationship they have with you. Respect their wishes.

UPDATES

If major donors have no objection to being recognized or to having further contact, then you should set up a system whereby you keep them updated on the project or program they support.

You might keep them informed through personal notes sent out quarterly. You might keep them apprised through monthly newsletters or emailed notices.

Fundraising leaders often don't realize that they are in partnership with donors. They are working as partners to accomplish a goal together. No one in a business partnership should take advantage of the other business partner, and the same applies to fundraising groups and their donor partners.

In addition to updates, it's also just fine to communicate with your donors on matters unrelated to fundraising:

> "Marie, Fr. Stevens is going to be visiting us next month. I know you've wanted to meet him. Want to get together for lunch while he's here?"

> "Hey Stan! I saw that your company got this year's Best of the Best Award. Wow! Good going!"

Quick little emails, texts, or phone calls such as these are great for maintaining contact.

APPROACHING DONORS AGAIN

If you've maintained communication with your donors throughout a major project, then you probably have learned some of their interests, likes, dislikes, and concerns. You've gotten to know them. You know what tugs at their heart strings. Maybe they have a special affection for the school's music program, or they remember fondly when the big stained glass window was installed, or they became best friends with Msgr. Grayson before he died.

If a new project comes up in your parish that might appeal to these interests, then by all means, let your donors know. Perhaps the school music program needs money to expand, or the stained glass window needs some costly repairs, or your parish is starting the Msgr. Grayson fund for seminarians. Make sure you know all you can about the new project before you mention this to the potential donors and let them know how they can help.

CHAPTER 10
PRESENTING THE NEED

"Oh, it'll cost a million dollars."

A few years ago, a parish manager asked me about writing grant proposals to fund a convent renovation. I asked him how much the renovation would cost. He said, "Oh, it'll cost a million dollars." Now, I know that *nothing* costs exactly one million dollars, so I asked him where he got that amount. He told me that a contractor had looked over the convent and announced that it was a million-dollar project. The parish manager had no bids, no schedule of materials, no estimates from electricians or plumbers, no cost breakdowns, nothing.

I told the manager that I could not help him—and that no one was likely to donate—until he had more details. He refused to budge; he already had that million-dollar amount in his head. That conversation took place more than five years ago. To this day, no one has ever pulled together the actual renovation costs, and the convent is still sitting there, untouched.

It's important to thoroughly assess and clearly present the need for which you are raising funds. In this chapter, we'll look at some small, medium, and large projects that need money, and we'll see how you might present the needs differently for each one. I won't define "small," "medium," or "large" as the definitions differ according to the size and wealth of different parishes. Each parish must define those terms for itself.

THE SMALL PROJECTS

Quite often, minor needs can be quickly defined. The church needs a wheelchair ramp, for example. Or the seats in the choir loft need to be re-upholstered. These may be small projects, but even minor fundraising efforts demand a certain amount of homework and a clear presentation of the need. For such projects, you might just include a paragraph in the church bulletin, a blurb on the parish web site, and an inclusion in the announcements before or after Masses. Or do all three, because different parishioners get their information through different channels. For your announcement, you need nothing more than this:

> **Help Us Get the Wheelchair Ramp!!** On the first and second Sundays in July (July 6 & 13), the Men's Club will be selling discounted tickets to the City Pool, Skating Rink, and Bowl-in-One to raise money for a wheelchair ramp. Concrete for the ramp costs $380 and one-day rental of a mixer is $67. All labor is donated and the ramp will be in place by mid-August. Help us make our church more accessible for everyone!!

This tells supporters everything they need to know—the cost, the timeframe, the sale dates, and the purpose. Also, the ticket sales are appropriate for summertime activities.

THE MEDIUM PROJECTS

Now let's look at some bigger projects. Perhaps the church needs new pews. Or the school's playground equipment should be replaced. Or the rectory needs a complete kitchen overhaul.

We'll take the playground project and see how it should be assessed. Before asking for money, the fundraising group should find out:

- How old is the existing equipment?
- Are the items beyond repair?
- Which pieces get the most use?
- Which pieces get the least use? Should those even be replaced?
- How much will each new item cost?
- Where will they be purchased?
- Has any money been raised so far?
- Can we get discounts?
- Will the equipment require special installation? If so, at what cost?
- Can members of the parish install the pieces?
- Has anyone agreed to do the installations?
- When will the pieces be installed? Over spring break? During the summer?

Next, the group should present their project in a clear and succinct way. They might insert a flyer into the church bulletin, distribute handouts at the next PTO meeting, or put the project details up on the parish's website.

HONEY, NOT VINEGAR

When presenting your request for medium or large projects, here's an important rule to follow. Present the need in a positive way, not a negative one. What do I mean by that?

Well, you've probably gotten those negative solicitation letters in the mail. "If we don't meet our $250,000 goal by March 1, we'll have to slash our programs to the bone." "In the time it takes you to read this letter, 43 more children will become homeless."

"Congress has ignored our pleas and now it's time to act!" I may truly feel for their cause, but instilling panic and fear in donors or potential donors is no way to attract or retain them.

So, looking at the playground equipment project, how can we give it a positive spin? One of the best things you can do is show that something's already been accomplished:

- Playground Heaven, Inc. has agreed to give us a 15% discount on equipment
- The school kids have raised $622 with their Pennies for Play drive
- The men's club has agreed to install the swing sets and slide
- A parishioner has already donated the cost of the monkey bars

Statements such as these will show donors that they're not starting from scratch, that parishioners are already contributing, and, perhaps most importantly, that the beneficiaries of the project have also been doing their part. Such a presentation is positive and upbeat. It gives donors hope that the project can be completed efficiently, on time, and without cost overruns.

CHAPTER 11
THE BIG PROJECTS

"Present the overall vision"

Sometimes, the parish has a much bigger project on the table—building a new rectory or buying and installing a new pipe organ, for example. For such projects, parishes often contract with fundraising firms to run a capital campaign or a pledge drive.

Alternatively, the pastor and parish council may decide not to contract out the fundraising and to handle everything in-house. Either way, someone must do plenty of homework in advance. (See the list below.) Until such homework is completed, you really cannot expect to get your fundraising off the ground.

WHAT A CAPITAL CAMPAIGN IS

A capital campaign is a program that aims to raise money for a specific well-defined need. Typically, the well-defined need involves the creation of new buildings or additions or improvements to existing buildings. However, in recent years, capital campaigns have broadened to include such things as the creation of endowments or development of entire, new service programs. Capital campaigns might last for several years and should not be conducted frequently. Some experts even suggest that there should be at least a 10-year wait between the end of the last campaign and the beginning of a new one.

WHAT'S INVOLVED UP FRONT

Whether your parish chooses to rely on its own people to run the campaign or to hire a fundraising company, there are certain things that your pastor, a building committee, the parish staff and/or qualified parishioners will still have to do before even getting started. Some of these tasks are listed below.

- Define exactly what you're raising money for. Don't just state that you need a new rectory; say that you need a new, 2-story, 3,200 square foot rectory with 4 bedrooms, 2 offices, a 4-car garage, and a basement.
- Obtain time and cost estimates from various architects, builders, contractors, artists, landscape designers, etc. for the project.
- Choose the professionals you intend to use and have them provide proposals, drawings, or whatever is necessary to help parishioners visualize the project.
- Based on their input, and considering possible cost overruns, determine your fundraising goal.
- Designate reasonable start and end dates for your campaign.
- Clean up your current member database or create a database if you don't have one already. Make sure you have the correct contact information for everyone.
- Be able to quickly identify your big donors, moderate donors, small donors, and non-donors.
- Be able to honestly communicate to others the need for the project, without exaggeration and without hiding anything.
- More than that, be able to communicate the long-term vision that is driving the project, how the finished project will better enable your church or school to fulfill its mission.

- Make sure your board is on board. Your parish council, finance council, building committee and/or school board should be behind the campaign 100% and be willing to contribute to the campaign in significant financial and non-financial ways.
- Ensure that you have the okay of the bishop and the diocesan building committee to undertake your capital project, to proceed with your capital campaign, and, if applicable, to use the fundraising firm you have chosen. Folks at the diocesan level may even suggest or require that you use a certain firm that has already been vetted and used by other parishes.

FEASIBILITY STUDIES

If the fundraising project is a particularly big one for your parish, or if your leadership feels "iffy" about running a campaign at all, then a feasibility study is a good idea. The study can show how likely it is you will meet your fundraising goal and, if so, what sort of deadline is reasonable. The study should be run by an outside consultant, possibly someone from a professional firm that runs capital campaigns. Again, you might get recommendations from some of the people at the diocesan level or from pastors of other churches that have run feasibility studies before their own capital campaigns.

During the feasibility study, the consultant will review your donor database and interview parishioners at every giving level in the parish. Keeping in mind the 80-20 rule—that 80% of your donations will come from 20% of your donors—the consultant will interview an inordinately large segment of your big donors. This expert may also interview past and present staff, volunteers, and others who are, or who have been, closely associated with the parish. He or she will also assess the likelihood that local corporations, foundations, and interested non-parishioners will contribute. With the consultant's report, your parish should be able to determine whether it's reasonable to proceed with the campaign.

CAMPAIGNS OPERATED BY OUTSIDE COMPANIES—THE SHORT VERSION

Companies that run capital campaigns each have their own way of handling things. This book is not intended to provide details on how such companies operate. But we can give a little preview of what you might expect.

From the pulpit, the pastor will announce and explain the need for the campaign. He should present the overall vision of why extraordinary funds are needed and how the capital project will enhance the parish or school's role in the lives of parishioners, students, and the community. He will tell how much money is to be raised and by when. He will also let parishioners know whether the parish is using an outside firm to run the campaign, and explain why that decision was made.

Next, the larger donors may be invited to attend a special event such as a steak dinner or a wine and cheese party with a string quartet. The pastor, associate pastor, parish council members, and school principal should also attend. At this event, there should be a very polished presentation on the importance of the church or school to the community, its historical significance, the generations it has served, and so forth. Once the donors are reminded of the many *relationships* that have developed from this parish or school, the presenter can address the need that the capital campaign will address. Donors might be given the opportunity to give at that time or to commit to give later. Some churches report that they have met more than 50% of their funding goal at these special, intimate events.

A bit later, another, less formal event might be conducted for all parishioners. This could be a barbecue, a catered meal, or a Thanksgiving dinner where the same polished presentation would be made. The pastor should speak about the campaign and pledge cards should be handed to everyone before they depart.

As soon as the checks begin arriving, the pastor should send personalized notes or letters of thanks to the donors. Even if these are standardized letters, each one should be hand-signed and include an individualized, hand-written sentence or two at the bottom. This does not need to be elaborate, just something like "Thanks, Liz, for your generous and quick response. You always come through for this parish!" Pastors who do this report that donors *really* respond to these personalized notes. Donors appreciate that they were recognized by more than a computer-generated form letter. (It may have something to do with relationships.) If some people choose to donate in installments, they should receive a letter with a personal note after each one.

As things proceed, it's absolutely necessary to keep thanking people and to keep apprising every one of the status of things. Even the small donations deserve a signed note of thanks. To keep everyone posted, you might include weekly announcements in the bulletin, special flyers when you hit milestones, or a parish party when you reach, say, the 80% mark.

The thanks notes and campaign updates serve to preserve the sense of ownership that donors have with the project. They also serve to maintain and strengthen the *relationships* that people have developed within their parish.

A fundraising company will help oversee and direct these events. But even if you hire a company, there are still certain tasks that your pastor and staff will have to undertake, especially those listed at the beginning of the chapter.

GOING IT ALONE

Now, some parishes will choose not to use a fundraising company. But one huge problem with trying to handle this alone is that it demands an enormous commitment of time and effort— sometimes for several years. Parish staff can become swamped with paperwork, income tracking, and database searching. People can will fall behind in their normal duties or find themselves chronically working overtime. Pledges can accidentally mix in with the normal weekly collections.

To avoid such headaches, I strongly recommend that a church temporarily hire an individual or a small team of parishioners (and non-parishioners if necessary) to handle everything. Team members should have experience with fundraising and business management. They should also be personable, communicate easily with donors, and commit to treating donors' information confidentially. They should have specific, defined roles. One person should be the team leader who keeps everything organized and running on schedule, and who reports to the pastor. These team members do not have to be fulltime employees but they should be fairly compensated for their time.

CHALLENGE GIFTS

If you have a parishioner who is likely to give a particularly large donation, say $10,000, the pastor should consider approaching that donor early in the campaign. The purpose here is two-fold. First, the pastor will talk to them about their gift and will thank them personally for their generosity. Second, he might ask them if he can use their donation as a "challenge" later when the campaign bogs down and donations are falling short. At that time, the pastor could announce that one donor is willing to match dollar-for-dollar all future donations up to a total of $10,000. Such a challenge could flush out even some of the most resistant donors.

All in all, a capital campaign is a huge undertaking. It can go on for years, but it can be made somewhat easier if you get fundraising experts involved. There are many websites that offer information and advice on capital campaigns, both from fundraising experts and from churches that have run campaigns. Just a few of these sites are listed below.

The Basics of a Capital Campaign
www.thenonprofitpartnership.org/files/cfd-campaign-basics-ppt.pdf

Church Capital Campaign Advice
http://charity.lovetoknow.com/Church_Capital_Campaign_Advice

How to Run a Successful Capital Campaign
http://www.nonprofitaccountingbasics.org/fundraising/how-run-successful-capital-campaign

Top Ten Reasons Why Campaigns Fail
http://www.capitalcampaigns.com/campaign_management/man
age_top_ten_reasons_campigns_fail.php

7 Keys to Successful Church Building Fund Capital Campaign Projects
http://www.kluth.org/church/7keys4bldgcampaigns.htm

CHAPTER 12
BREAKING OUT OF THE BOX

"how to buy...sell...research...patent...and lose weight"

By now, the way you think about fundraising should be quite different from how you perceived it at the beginning of the book. You should have a new appreciation for your volunteers and your donors. You might be thinking of ways to draw non-parishioners into your fundraising events. Perhaps you've even dropped the word "fundraiser" from these events.

Maybe you're dreaming up a list of items and services that people actually want or need. You are thinking of ways to capitalize on these to create steady income streams. For instance, you might be thinking of different classes your parishioners could offer during the coming year. Or maybe you're thinking of ways to enhance the end-of-semester survival baskets for college students.

When you stop beating the fundraiser drum and start offering needed, wanted services and items, you accomplish three things. First, you improve relationships with your donors. People look forward to seeing what your group is offering next. They see your creativity as refreshing. They come to rely on you to provide something worth having.

Second, new relationships crop up among parishioners. Those who purchase other parishioners' services at auction will likely make new friends. Retired folks who come to the furniture refinishing class will get to know others who share their interests. Kids who put together the **Dates to Remember** calendar will meet almost everyone in the parish.

Third, your parish's relationship with the community is enhanced. It's likely that your church already has great relationships with a handful of other organizations. Perhaps the parish donates canned goods every month to a food pantry. Maybe it contributes a certain amount quarterly to a homeless shelter. The parish might always buy soft drinks and snack trays from the same grocery store. But imagine if your parish became known as the best place to take Spanish classes, or held the best barbecue competition every spring. People throughout the community would recognize such good contributions and start showing up.

Most of us think of fundraising as single-event or single-campaign efforts. We also tend to think of fundraising as confined to our own parish or, at best, to the local Catholic community. In Chapters 3 and 4, though, we began looking a little beyond those confines. We started to see where we had potential to attract people from outside of the parish and we began to offer activities to a wider audience.

Now we're going to consider taking bigger leaps and looking farther into the future. We are going to no longer see fundraising activities as fundraising activities. We're going to see them as things our parish just does.

THINKING BEYOND THE PARISH

Many of the fundraising ideas in this book have focused on events or activities intended to attract parishioners. But certain others were set up to attract people from outside. If we start to think even bigger, we can come up with ideas to attract supporters from throughout your city, your diocese, or even your state. Let's look at a couple of possibilities.

Professional seminars

You've probably seen the hyped-up ads for those seminars that sweep into town. They involve a day or two at a rented meeting room in a local hotel. A speaker or promoter supposedly teaches the audience how to make money in real estate or investments or selling products online. The seminars cost hundreds of dollars. Or else they're free, but attendees are pressured to spend hundreds of dollars on books and CDs and DVDs. Some of the seminar topics may be quite good, but the hype and the pressure imply that audiences are being taken for a ride.

In earlier chapters, we discussed the parishioners with untapped talent and expertise. Let's expand on that idea. If there are attorneys, building contractors, engineers, physicians, or other professionals in your parish, you might ask them if they'd offer a seminar in their field. Some ideas might include:

- How to buy and flip houses
- What you should know about interior design
- How to be the building contractor for your own renovation project
- Mistakes to avoid in buying your first home
- Great new ideas for landscaping
- Growing your own vegetables in a small space
- How to present your products to the television shopping networks
- How to start a retail business in your state
- How to patent an invention
- How to build an effective website for your company or service
- How to market your new product over the Internet
- Selling on Amazon, ebay, etsy, and other sites

- Planning a fabulous wedding while keeping costs under control
- How to find grants
- How to set up your will, trust, or estate
- What to know about living wills, healthcare proxies, and advanced directives
- How to choose a retirement center or assisted living facility
- Ways to get your book published
- How to research your family tree
- How to avoid the biggest investment pitfalls
- How to take advantage of the latest tax breaks
- How to start a nonprofit organization
- How to lose weight, according to the latest research
- Effectively managing your diabetes
- Best methods for keeping your brain active and alert as you age
- Creating the most effective resume
- Job and hiring possibilities that are often overlooked
- Tracking down college scholarships

Some of these seminars might go on for several days, while others would take up only an afternoon or evening. Every seminar should be pressure-free, highly informative, and above reproach. No instructor would be allowed to promote his or her own company or services. And no supplemental materials would be available for sale. Advertisements for the seminars should state that these are pressure-free events and that no other materials will be promoted or sold before, during, or afterwards. Attendees would be charged a reasonable fee and presenters would be fairly compensated for their time.

After only a couple of seminars, your parish would have a reputation for offering something highly valuable to the entire community. While your parish might already be known for assisting the local food pantry or battered women's shelter, now it would be recognized for providing services to people from all walks of life. That is, in addition to already doing it in the spiritual realm.

Meeting Parishioner and Church Needs

Perhaps a fundraising group in your parish could sell a product or service that churches or parishioners all throughout the diocese could use. For example, during any 12-month period, Catholics or their schools or parishes across the diocese will buy:

- Small candles with holders for Easter Vigil services
- 1-week vigil lights
- Lilies at Easter
- Poinsettias at Christmas
- Replacement altar linens
- Replacement surplices for altar servers
- Baptismal gifts
- First Communion veils and dresses
- Gifts for First Communicants
- Gifts for Confirmandi
- In Filipino parishes, gifts for Debut
- In Hispanic parishes, gifts for Quinceanera
- School uniforms
- Clothing and items with imprinted or embroidered school mascots or logos

Maybe a group within your parish could begin creating (or growing) just one of these items. The group could sell the items within the parish for the first few years, then expand to other parishes in later years.

Take the Communion veils, for example. Let's say 3,000 children in your diocese made their First Communion last year. (You can get the actual number from your diocesan office.) Of that 3,000, about 1,500 were little girls wearing veils. Now, my own online search of Communion veils revealed prices ranging from $14 to $130, with most in the $30 to $50 range. Imagine. If all 1,500 girls wore the $14 veils, that's $21,000 spent on veils in one year.

Many parishes have craft guilds or ladies' sewing groups. Certainly, creative and talented folks from such groups could design and make veils at a reasonable cost and sell them to parishioners. In time, they could develop a business plan for spreading the sales to other, nearby parishes, throughout the entire diocese, or even nationally through an online store.

Someone in the parish could develop a promotional brochure complete with photos and prices, and send them to Directors of Religious Education throughout the diocese. All promotional materials should state that proceeds from the sales go to benefit needy families, seminarians, or whomever your fundraising group supports.

ADVERTISING

I've mentioned advertising a number of times in this book and it's the professional seminars mentioned earlier that could especially benefit from widespread promotion. Below, I suggest a few ways that you can get the word out and do it for free.

- Local cable companies are often required to provide public access channels where schools, churches, and organizations can publicize their events. Just give them a call and ask their advertising manager how to get some air time for your event.

- Diocesan newspapers and magazines have "around the diocese" columns that publicize upcoming fundraisers.
- Radio and television stations generally run Public Service Announcements (PSAs) for nonprofits. These are free, but they might run at odd hours like 3:00 a.m. and in the middle of a pile of other PSAs. Still, it's advertising.
- Newspapers accept press releases from churches that are putting on special events. Press releases have a certain format though, so search online for "press release format" before you submit anything. You'll find some differences between formats, but they all have features in common. Once you write and format your release, make sure someone else checks it over before you submit it to the newspaper.

A WORD ABOUT DEVELOPMENT DIRECTORS

Before I wind up, I want to say something about development directors. Many parishes and dioceses hire DDs to oversee or run their major fundraising programs. In most cases, this just becomes a total burnout job. The DD is often expected to wear many hats and change personalities like a chameleon changes color.

He must be the serious, thoughtful person who speaks to large donors about planned giving via their wills or bequests. She must be the outgoing, Type A personality who whips up interest for every fundraiser that comes along. The DD must be an adept grant writer who beats deadlines and is willing to speak with or meet with foundation directors. As soon as the DD is hired, he knows he has to bring in several times his own salary. Or she knows she's expected to direct several vastly different fundraising efforts, only to discover that the first one is already larger than one person can handle.

I have known several development directors, and each one had a job description that was impossible to meet. If your parish or school does choose to hire a DD, I suggest that your pastor and search committee first think about which income-generating activities they want that person to handle—finding grants, running the parish's fundraising events, expanding the number of regular donors, encouraging current donors to increase their level of giving, overseeing a capital campaign, or focusing on planned giving. They should prioritize these activities, knowing that no one person can do all things, and make the priorities plain to the job applicants.

In Summary

Okay, we've covered a lot of ground. But this is what my thousands of words boil down to:

Chapter 1: Behave
Chapter 2: Relationships, relationships, relationships
Chapter 3: Take out the garbage
Chapters 4 and 5: Improve what remains
Chapter 6: Open your eyes
Chapter 7: Honor thy volunteers
Chapter 8: Get to know your donors
Chapter 9: Respect them
Chapters 10 and 11: Understand the fundraising need
Chapter 12: Try new things and be not afraid

And one more thing: Have fun!

Index

About the Author

Susan H. Gray has been a writer for longer than she can remember. In graduate school (MS in Zoology), her major professor was also the editor of a peer-reviewed scientific journal. Through their association, Susan was blessed to learn much about the processes of writing, editing, and publishing.

Eventually, she became a contract writer for a number of children's educational book publishers. She currently has more than 150 books in print, mainly for K-6 readers, and primarily on scientific topics.

Susan also spent two years as a technical writer for medical device and pharmaceutical companies. In 1993, she began working as a writer of grant proposals for a medical school. That same year, she discovered—and began volunteering with—the Mary Mother of God Mission Society, a Catholic organization dedicated to reviving the Catholic Church in Eastern Russia. At that time, she began writing grant proposals for the society and also became heavily involved in parish fundraising for the mission work.

More than two decades later, Susan remains active as a grant writer, primarily for the mission society, although she has also written for a number of other Catholic organizations. She continues her work with parish fundraising and sees many parallels between the two endeavors.

Susan lives in Cabot, Arkansas, with her husband Michael and many pets.

www.ingramcontent.com/pod-product-compliance
Lightning Source LLC
Chambersburg PA
CBHW070940210326
41520CB00021B/6981